Tears of Sadness
Tears of Joy

Tears of Sadness
Tears of Joy

One Couple's Journey Through
Love, Faith, and Mental Illness

Jo Vamos Honig

White River Press
Amherst, Massachusetts

First published in 2020 by White River Press
PO Box 3561, Amherst, MA 01004 • www.whiteriverpress.com

Cover and Book Design by Lufkin Graphic Designs
Norwich, Vermont • www.lufkingraphics.com

Cover image from a 1960s view of Elkhart, Indiana, postcard from
http://www.papergreat.com/2015_08_16_archive.html

ISBN: 978-1-887043-65-6 paperback
       978-1-887043-66-3 ebook

Unless otherwise indicated, all Scripture quotations in this publication are taken from the New King James Version®. Copyright © 1982 by Thomas Nelson. Used by permission. All rights reserved.

Scripture quotation marked "Phillips" is taken from The New Testament in Modern English, ©1958, 1959, 1960, 1972, J. B. Phillips, and 1947, 1952, 1955, 1957, the Macmillan Company, New York. Used by permission. All rights reserved.

Library of Congress Cataloging-in-Publication Data

Names: Honig, Jo, 1937- author.
Title: Tears of sadness, tears of joy / Jo Honig.
Description: Amherst, Massachusetts : White River Press, 2020. |
Identifiers: LCCN 2019053481 (print) | LCCN 2019053482 (ebook) | ISBN
    9781887043663 (ebook) | ISBN 9781887043656 (trade paperback) | ISBN
    9781887043656¬q(trade paperback) | ISBN 9781887043663¬q(ebook)
Subjects: LCSH: Vamos, Bill--Mental health. | Honig, Jo, 1937- |
    Manic-depressive persons--Indiana--Biography. |
    Clergy--Indiana--Biography. | Husband and wife--Indiana.
Classification: LCC RC516.B5125 (ebook) | LCC RC516.B5125 H66 2020 (print) |
    DDC 616.89/50092 [B] --dc23
LC record available at https://lccn.loc.gov/2019053481

Dedication

To Bill Vamos, a man of strength and courage
who never gave up and who taught me to live and love
even when life hurts.

Author's Note

On his deathbed my husband, Bill Vamos, asked me to finish the manuscript he had started. He wanted the world to know that even being born with mental illness, one can lead a full, productive life. This book is an intermingling of our stories. Bill started the manuscript and I added details to his chapters as I imagined them to have happened. Some of the chapters are from his point of view, some from my own. The heart-wrenching description of his time in the hospital is solely his writing, based on his accurate recall.

Through it all, it was Bill's faith that helped to sustain him. Although I lost Bill to cancer in 1994, through this book I am able to interweave our voices to tell the many stories of our life together. I have done my best to stay true to Bill's voice, and also to his hope for this book: that it shows, through sharing his journey, how a life with mental illness can still be a life full of meaningful work, deep love, and enduring faith.

Prologue

Jo

MY HAND TREMBLED as I gripped the doorknob of the hospital room. How could my husband have ended up here again?

After taking a deep breath to steel my nerves, I opened the door. A vague hint of daylight pushed through the steel bars stretched across the lone window, but it did little to dispel the darkness.

Bill lay curled up in the fetal position on a mattress on the floor, asleep. Though this was the fourth time I'd seen him in a place like this, I still shuddered at the sight. I thought my heart would explode, leaving pieces of it scattered around the stark room.

There was nothing I could say that would reach him. So, I did the only thing I could think of. I laid myself directly on top of his sweat-soaked body. I whispered in his ear, reminding him how much I loved him and how much God loved him.

I lay there for a long time, silently crying out for God to hear me, to heal him, and to stop the madness. *Why is this wonderful husband of mine in such pain? He crashed so hard this time. What has he done to deserve this?* He was doing all the right things: taking his meds, exercising, journaling, and praying. I wondered what might have triggered this episode. Exhaustion, probably, with Christmas three weeks away, and all the programs and responsibilities at the church.

Or could I be at fault? For the past four weeks, as I prepared to sing a lead role in Handel's *Solomon*, I needed constant reassurance from Bill. I was excited about singing with the Elkhart orchestra, but I wasn't sure I could do it well. Bill knew that if my performance wasn't flawless, I would berate myself mercilessly. And he had lovingly reassured me, time and again, that I was not a failure.

I'd been so focused on myself lately, I failed to notice my husband was taking more sleeping pills than usual. Until I found him here, in the psych ward.

Chapter One

Bill

1

S TEPHANIE GRANT, with her sweet Southern drawl, was the catch of the campus. And I, Bill Vamos, was deeply in love with her. What I loved most about this second-year sociology major at Hanover College was how much she loved me. Every Saturday night, we'd slip into the most secluded booth at our favorite diner, the Hanover Campus Cabin, where we sipped chocolate milk shakes and necked until manager Mike Scroggins blinked the lights on and off. Whenever I sat in my classes, or worked at my campus laundry-and-trash-collection job, I would fall into a sort of stupor, just thinking about her model-like legs and her curvaceous body.

As I lay in my bunk, staring at the bottom of the cot above me, I recalled Stephanie's luminous blue eyes and her golden hair glistening in the moonlight as I had slipped my fraternity ring on her finger earlier that evening. I had made my frat brothers rehearse for forty-five minutes, hoping their serenade would clinch the deal. It worked—she said yes! After I drove her home, my friends got their revenge by tying me to the front fender of my work truck and pushing it into the Ohio River. Soon after I hit the water they pulled it back to dry land. But, sewage and all, I felt like I'd won the lottery that night. It was only later that I paid for that smelly ride in the Ohio River, when soon after, my sinuses exploded.

I had wondered sometimes if my fraternity brothers were envious of me, thinking I had it all. Little did they know I envied them. They knew nothing of the inner demons that constantly threatened to overwhelm me.

I rolled over in my bunk bed and wrapped the thin pillow around my head, trying to drown out the sound of my fraternity brothers' snoring and heavy breathing. Seconds after they fell into bed, they all slipped into delicious slumber. I was lucky if I slept at all.

Some of my friends weren't as smart as I was. Most drank too much. One of them had shacked up with every loose woman on campus. But I'd trade my life with any one of them in an instant.

My nerves kept me awake, like an army of needles marching inside me, sticking my stomach, arms, and chest, all at the same time. I repeatedly told myself to relax. But that only intensified the attack. I tried to picture something pleasant: Michigan, Northern pike, Mom's coffee cake, my beautiful Stephanie. Nothing helped.

To make matters worse, the sinusitis I'd battled my entire adult life ballooned my face and clamped my eyelids almost shut. Pain exploded in every cavity of my head.

I needed help. But none of my friends could do anything for me. When morning finally came, I climbed out of bed, then just stood there by my bunk, mentally paralyzed. When my roommates realized something was seriously wrong, my buddy Bob Delany drove me to my parents' home in Cincinnati.

The minute I stumbled through the front door the color drained from my mother's face. I walked past her to the living room and collapsed on Dad's recliner. Mom followed me. "What's wrong, Bill?"

I couldn't answer her. Weeks without sleep had left my mind confused, in a fog that refused to lift. But through the confusion I could smell, see, and feel what was happening around me. Out of my mother's immaculate kitchen emanated smells of freshly baked coffee cakes, ready to be shared with neighbors and sick friends.

I heard Mother running to the kitchen phone, where she called Dad's office at the national headquarters of the Kroger Company. "Frank, something is wrong with our son. His friend Bob brought him home from Hanover. He's very sick. Please come home as soon as possible. He needs our help."

After she hung up, Bob took her arm and led her to the green sofa in the living room. Her small frame trembled as she leaned against the arm of the sofa, her face pale, like a faded painting.

A half hour later Dad came running through the front door, his six-foot frame slightly bent from a bicycle accident he had as a teen. He quickly brought in a chair from the dining room and joined Mother and Bob. I couldn't hear much of their whispered conversation, but I knew my friend was explaining to my parents what he saw happening to me at Hanover. When he finished, the three of them came to where I was sitting.

Bob reached for my hand. "I have to get back to school. But I'll see you when you're feeling better."

All I could say was "Thank you."

Mom and Dad walked him to the door and returned quickly to see how I was doing. I tried to stand, but my body shook so fiercely that Dad had to ease me back into the recliner. He pulled up a footstool and sat close to me, his deep brown eyes gazing at me with empathy. "Son, what is happening to you?"

I tried to use what little strength I had to explain to my parents how I'd lost my ability to concentrate on my studies or even to carry on a conversation. That I had to stop going to classes because I couldn't sit still. But my words got all tangled up. I knew my mother was silently praying while I talked; that's what Mom did.

In an attempt to relieve the pain from my sinusitis, I lowered my face to my knees and rocked back and forth. Mom choked on a sob. "Frank, I believe our son is having a mental breakdown."

A mental breakdown? Did that mean I was crazy? The room started to spin, like a carousel out of control.

Dad's body collapsed into the chair beside me as if someone had punched him. He took my shoulders and gently raised my torso till we were face-to-face. "Son, I'm going to call Pastor Shultz and see if he knows the name of a doctor who can help you."

I couldn't think beyond the pain. But I knew I needed help. After I nodded my approval, Dad left to make the phone call. I leaned back in the recliner, Mother hovering nearby.

After what felt like a long time, my father returned, his face flushed. "I told Pastor Shultz what's happening to you, Bill. He believes a psychiatrist is needed. He gave me the name of a local one." Dad's jaw tightened. "I called the psychiatrist's office and talked with his nurse. I gave her a few of the details. She said she would talk to the doctor and he would call me back." My father took a deep breath. "He called back within fifteen minutes. He asked a lot of questions."

Dad looked down at the green carpet, seemingly reluctant to go on. Finally, he looked up toward the ceiling, took a deep breath, then lowered his head slowly. "Bill, the doctor would like to admit you to the hospital today. The nurse has reserved a room for you at Good Samaritan."

Today? Things were happening too fast.

Dad searched my face. "Are you ready to go to the hospital, and possibly to the psychiatric ward?"

Panic set in. "Will I be there . . . forever?"

"No, son. This is a place where people get well."

I looked my dad in the eye. "I—I guess I'll go."

I had never seen my father cry. But tears bubbled up. He turned away and started toward the basement door, mumbling about getting the car. Mom, tears streaming down her face, hurried to my room to collect clothes and toiletries. I sat there, wondering if I would ever be well again.

When Mom was ready, we made our way to the garage, where Dad waited in his brand-new Chrysler. I sprawled across the backseat. No one spoke on the ride to the hospital. Dad sat tall in the driver's seat, periodically checking the map. Mom's small frame disappeared in the passenger seat.

We arrived at the hospital around 3:00. The parking lot was a sea of cars, but we managed to find a spot near the entrance. The impressive brick building had hundreds of windows, all staring at me.

When we got out of the car, Mom took my arm. With Dad behind us, we walked into the hospital. The lobby was brightly lit and spacious, with couches scattered throughout. Some people paced, others sat. Children played at the feet of their parents. We walked to the information desk in the middle of the room. A white-haired woman looked up and smiled. "May I help you?"

Dad leaned over the high counter. Moving close to her ear, he whispered, "We're looking for the psychiatric wing."

Mother led me to one of the couches. I sat there, shaking, until Dad walked over to us and said, "Follow me." He gently took my arm and lifted me from the couch. The three of us walked down a long hallway, the walls lined with brightly colored contemporary paintings. We turned left at the end of the hall and saw a nondescript door with a sign that said PSYCHIATRIC WING. On the other side of the hall was another waiting room. Though the room was well lit, its wood paneling and maroon carpeting made it feel dark. A few functional chairs lined the walls. The air smelled like citrus disinfectant.

Behind the counter sat a young woman with red hair and bright red fingernail polish. "May I help you?"

Mother stepped forward. "Dr. Kline recommended—" She couldn't continue.

Dad took over. "Our son is ill." He inhaled a sketchy breath. "The doctor recommended he spend some time in the psychiatric ward."

With a knowing nod, the receptionist picked up the phone. After she hung up, she turned to my father. "Your doctor phoned a little while ago with an order to admit your son. There's a lot of paperwork, but that can be done later. Why don't you take a seat. The nurse will be here in a little while."

My parents and I sat in adjoining chairs. Mom put her arms around me. Her warm body felt like an oasis in the midst of a vast desert. We waited without saying a word. I kept shaking, chills of panic running down my spine. *There's no turning back now.* I wondered if the folks here thought I was crazy.

The clock above the high desk indicated that we had been sitting for fifteen minutes when a tall, slender woman came through the double doors, her wheat-colored hair tucked neatly into a starched white cap. She smiled as she shook my hand. "Hello, Bill," she cooed. "I'm Nurse Linowski. I understand you'll be staying with us for a while."

I stared at her, in too much pain to respond. "Yes, he will," my parents answered simultaneously.

Nurse Linowski took my arm. "All right, Bill. Come with me."

We walked down a long hall, my parents following. When we reached a closed door, she turned to them. "I'm sorry, Mr. and Mrs. Vamos, but you can't come any farther. You can call tomorrow and see how he's doing."

My father nodded. My mother hugged me tight, tears dripping down her cheeks. I felt numb. I couldn't take on her pain. I had too much of my own.

After unlocking the door, Nurse Linowski led me down a shorter hall to a small, windowless room with a bed, a chair, and a closet. She pulled a clipboard out of the plastic pouch hanging outside the door. Pen poised above the top sheet of paper she asked a series of questions. I tried to answer her, but anxiety and physical pain blocked my memory. When she realized there was nothing more she could learn, she returned my chart to the pouch and left, closing the door behind her.

I collapsed onto the bed, trapped in a world of emotional and physical pain. I felt like a grown-up fetus waiting to be born.

2

Day after day, I lay on my hospital bed, barely breathing, afraid that my heartbeat would awaken more pain. A blur of faces and voices came and went. Time had no meaning. Eventually, the drugs the doctor had prescribed started working. The fog in my head began to lift, and my physical pain diminished slightly.

Around 8:00 a.m. one morning, I was sitting on the side of the bed when the door opened. In walked a stately looking man wearing a white coat and a stethoscope around his neck. "Good morning, Bill. I'm Dr. Kline. I've been overseeing your treatments." He shook my hand.

I didn't even recognize this man, who had been my physician for—how long had I been here? A few days? A week? Two weeks?

"How are you feeling, Bill?"

"Better, but not ready to run a marathon."

Dr. Kline smiled and wrote something in his chart. "You've had a tough time. But the sinusitis seems to be clearing, and the swelling has gone down. I'm glad to see you're improving." He picked up a small metal tube with a light on one end and peered inside my nasal passages. "Looks good. The nurses say you're eating better."

I nodded. I didn't remember eating anything those first few days. But I could recall having dinner the night before. The chicken and fries tasted better than anything I'd ever eaten.

"Your parents have come to see you a number of times, but the medications had you too drugged to be aware of their visits. You can call them back whenever you wish."

As soon as he left, I slipped out of bed and shuffled down the hall to the nurse's station. Dad would be at work, but I wanted to talk to my mother. A cute, dark-haired nurse helped me dial.

"Hi, Mom."

"Bill!" Her voice broke.

"I'm feeling better."

Silence.

"The doctor is encouraged."

"I'm so glad." She took a deep breath. "Can we come visit you tonight?"

I asked the nurse, then said, "Visiting hours are from seven thirty to nine thirty."

"We'll be there."

The visit that night was difficult. The medications had thickened my speech, so I slurred some of my words. But I was happy to see my parents. We all tried hard to make it a happy time.

Several days later, Nurse Linowski entered my room, her face beaming. She slipped a small but bulging manila envelope into my hand. "Smells like it's from a girl." She winked, then walked out the door.

I raised the package to my face and inhaled the faint whisper of Stephanie's perfume. I opened it with trembling fingers, excited to think that my girlfriend had sent me a get-well gift. I carefully unwrapped the tissue paper. My heart sank. All that was inside was my silver-and-gold fraternity ring. There wasn't even a note of explanation.

I wanted to scream and beat on the bed frame. But the slightest movement of my head would send spasms of pain everywhere. With an involuntary shiver, I dropped the envelope to the floor and returned to my curled-up position. *You're falling over the edge this time.*

I tried to recall happy moments with Steph during those last days at Hanover College. But in my mind's eye, all I could see was Bob Delany taking me by the hand and leading me out of the frat house to his '51 Pontiac.

"You saw that, didn't you?" I asked out loud, imagining Steph in front of me. "I don't blame you for wanting to turn away from that human robot, for deciding to forget him and hold on to the good times. I forgive you for losing track of the way we used to be."

The Stephanie in my vision did not respond.

"I'm going to make it out of this place," I promised her. "And when I do, I'll show you how strong I am. I'll give you the ring again, this time forever."

Nurse Linowski came in and injected me with something that caused instant sleep.

The next morning, she attached electrodes to my temples with some kind of gooey gel. The devices stunned my brain with lighting-hot electric shock, a tiny light into my confused darkness. Every morning the nurse administered this torture, letting me writhe for hours, hoping to shake me into thinking clearly.

Finally, the electric shock treatments began to work and my sinuses cleared up completely. I felt human again.

On Friday morning at 8:00, Dr. Kline burst through my hospital-room door. Without his usual "Good morning" greeting, he walked up to my bed and asked, "Are you ready to go home?"

I swung my legs off the bed and stood. I'd been eagerly waiting to hear that question. But was I ready to leave the protected environment of the hospital? I hadn't thought about what my life would be like outside. But now I had to come to grips with what came next for me. My future felt blank.

I looked at the doctor. "I—I think so."

"Well, you'll be leaving tomorrow morning. Your folks will pick you up. You'll need to work with a psychiatrist as an outpatient. I will discuss that with your parents."

I nodded. The idea of seeing a psychiatrist was about as foreign to the Vamos family as flying to the moon. But I knew I needed to talk to someone.

He smiled, then left the room.

I was going home! But my happiness was muted by fear of what lay ahead.

On a rainy Saturday morning in March, I packed my toothbrush, pajamas, and electric razor. Right at 9:00, after a light tap at the door, my parents walked in. They each gave me a long hug, then Mom helped me finish packing. Dad sat on the bed, waiting.

Nurse Linowski breezed into the room without knocking. She threw her arms around me and hugged me tightly. "The staff all wish you the very best. We're going to miss you." With a twinkle in her eye she added, "But we don't want to see you in here again!"

"I don't want to be back here ever again. But thank you for all you've done for me."

After another hug, she turned and left. The doctor arrived around 9:30. He shook hands with my parents. "Big day today!"

They nodded. I wondered if they knew how scary this was for me. I still needed to sort out many issues. What had happened to me and why? What did this mean for my future?

When Dr. Kline told my parents that he had made an appointment for me with Dr. Jacobson, one of Cincinnati's most renowned psychiatrists, I breathed a sigh of relief.

Mom chirped all the way home from the hospital. "What would you like to eat when we get home? What sounds good to you? How about some of Aunt Helen's *kuchen*? We're so thankful you're coming home. Aren't we, Frank?"

Dad kept his eyes on the road. "Yes, Vi, we are."

All I could think about was Stephanie, the way the wind blew her blonde hair when she walked through the campus, and her soft but passionate kisses. I wondered if I could win her back.

Should I call her?

No. As much as I ached for her, I wasn't strong enough, physically or mentally, to risk another rejection.

When we returned home, Mom hurried up the basement stairs and went straight to her kitchen to make a chicken casserole. After watching her preparations for a few minutes, I followed Dad into the living room. I collapsed onto the green couch while he settled into his leather recliner and picked up his pipe and newspaper.

It felt good to be home where Mom could pamper me. She was the quintessential homemaker; her mission in life was to make her family happy. And I loved her for it.

"Lunch is ready," she called from the kitchen. I had eaten hospital food for a month and a half, and Mom's home cooking tasted like a banquet.

"What would Dad and I do without you, Mom?"

Her face reddened a bit. "I do enjoy cooking. Besides, you lost so much weight, we need to put some meat on your bones."

Dad gave Mom a loving smile.

The morning had been tiring, and my body felt heavy with weariness. After finishing my ice cream and strawberries, I excused myself and headed down the hall.

My bedroom hadn't changed since I left for college. The bedspread was still red and blue with ships on it. The maple desk and dresser were organized just as I'd left them. I crawled under the covers and fell asleep.

Sleeping and eating were about all I did until my appointment on Thursday with Dr. Jacobson. Dad was at work most of the day and part of the evening, while Mom and I had many talks. But I couldn't share with her my deepest feelings. I would have to save those for Dr. Jacobson.

Thursday arrived sooner than I wished. My parents felt I still needed someone to drive for me. Mom had never learned to drive, and Dad had to work that day. Fortunately, Bob Delany, who lived in Cincinnati, was home for the week. He agreed to drive me to the doctor's office. Around 8:15 a.m., the doorbell rang. Mother ran to open it, then greeted Bob with a kiss on his cheek. When he saw me, he hurried over and slapped me on the back, then gave me a quick hug. "Hey, man, I'm glad you're feeling better."

A tear escaped from my eyes as I remembered how sick I was the last time Bob saw me. "Thanks for driving today."

"I'm happy to do it."

I gave Mom a hug and a kiss, and we left. All the way to the hospital I wondered what it would be like to talk to a psychiatrist. I'd never thought this was something I would have to do. And I wanted to talk to this doctor. I needed to tell him about Stephanie and what had happened to me. And ask what had caused this breakdown.

"Where's the parking garage?" Bob asked.

"It's in the basement of the bank building." The lot was almost empty, so we easily found a spot near the elevator.

On the third floor, we found a door labeled "Robert Jacobson, MD." I was relieved not to see the word *psychiatrist* next to his name.

The waiting room was comfortably furnished with thick wall-to-wall carpeting and cloth chairs. Bright paintings of sunflowers and poppies hung on the walls. A large clock read 8:55. Bob sat down and picked up a magazine while I walked over to the reception area. A young woman with dark roots under her bleached spiked hair slid open a glass window and asked my name.

"Bill Vamos."

While she looked at my chart, I leaned closer and whispered, "I'm here to see Dr. Jacobson. My appointment is for nine o'clock."

She looked up and smiled. "He's ready to see you. You can go right in." She pointed to his office.

When I opened the door, I saw a man in a brown suede jacket with dark hair and a full beard sprinkled with white, sitting behind a desk. He stood and held out his hand to shake mine. "Good morning. I'm Dr. Jacobson. Won't you have a seat?" He motioned to a leather armchair that swiveled.

This man wasn't at all what I had expected. He looked . . . normal. And peaceful.

Heavy oak shelf units held hardback books and cultural artifacts, and oil paintings lined the walls. Surrounded by art and books, two things I loved, I slowly began to release the tensions that had held me captive for such a long time.

The doctor adjusted his horn-rimmed glasses, and smiled at

me. "How are you feeling today, Bill?"

"Fine." After a few more generic questions, he asked, "What do you remember about your childhood?"

I looked just over his head at a painting of two people in a fishing boat, laughing as they pulled in their catch. "Not very much." I sank farther into the soft leather chair. In the hospital, when Nurse Linowski asked me about my early childhood, I couldn't remember a thing. She told me that electric shock treatments often blurred memories of the past.

When he scratched his head, I muttered, "I can't think. I miss Stephanie too much."

He swiveled his chair to the side. "Then tell me about her."

Though I hadn't felt comfortable even thinking about Stephanie until that moment, I spent the remainder of the session talking about her, looking down at my unpolished Florsheim shoes. It felt good to sort through my feelings with someone who would listen to me without judging me or uttering platitudes like "Everything will be all right."

Dr. Jacobson asked a few insightful questions, and his accepting smile encouraged me to continue talking. At the end of the hour I felt better. I was eager to see him again.

I visited Dr. Jacobson's office every Monday and Thursday. I liked this man of few words, with his dry sense of humor. I soon came to trust him. He never made me feel as if what I had to say was unimportant, and I came to realize that I could talk about anything without fear of rejection.

About three weeks into my sessions with Dr. J, he clasped his hands over the shiny mahogany desktop and announced, "Young man, I've arranged for you to spend two days with Stephanie at her home in Alabama."

I bolted upright in my chair. "How did you manage that?" I had called her several times to ask if I could see her, and she refused to even discuss it.

"Your parents gave me the number. She agreed to a short visit. Her family will pay for you to stay at a nearby motel."

I couldn't believe I was actually going to see Stephanie. Could I win her back? Would she realize how much I still loved her?

Again, Bob Delany came to my rescue. He loaned me his car so I could drive the 600 miles to Montgomery, which I did in less than nine hours.

I knocked on Stephanie's door, and she answered, beautiful as ever, smelling of lavender. Her hair was wet from the shower and her face flushed. I reached for her, wanting to pull her close, but she greeted me with a quick, friendly hug.

She spent the next two days showing me Montgomery's Civil War sites. Her ongoing narrative about all the historic points of interest left no time for talking about anything personal. It hurt to think that I was just a distraction in her life, not a person she cared about.

When we returned to her home on the last evening, I sat beside her on the living room couch, hoping we could rekindle our love. But she immediately escaped to a nearby chair. We sat in silence for several minutes. Finally, she looked me in the eye for the first time since I arrived. "We're just friends, Bill, no more. You've got to know that."

Her words stung. I wanted to fall on my knees and beg her to love me. But as I gazed into her eyes, I saw fear in them. I reached for her arm, determined to show her she had nothing to be afraid of. But she flinched at my touch and scurried out the door. My chest ached as though my heart were literally breaking. But I didn't follow her. It was over between us, and I had to accept that.

Back in Dr. J's office, I told him what happened on my visit with Stephanie.

"That must have been terribly hard for you."

No kidding.

Then he asked a strange question. "Does Stephanie resemble your mother?"

"Of course not!" I'd never heard anything so absurd. "Stephanie is passionate and sexy. My mother wears long dresses to cover her varicose veins. She never really kisses Dad, just smooches him, and sometimes me too. Tastes like stale lipstick and fried chicken."

Dr. J's raised eyebrows made me realize how my diatribe sounded.

"Mom's beautiful, though, in her own way. She's always visiting nursing homes, writing letters for sick people, baking coffee cakes for friends and neighbors. And her meals are masterpieces."

Dr. J peered at me. "Is Stephanie a good cook?"

I chuckled. "She can't boil water without burning the pan. But Steph is tender and sensitive. And you should see her in a pair of shorts."

Dr. J did not look amused. "How do your parents feel about her?"

"Dad likes her, but I think she's too sexy for Mom. They invited her for a weekend once, when our relationship started getting serious. I guess they wanted to see if she was wholesome enough for their son. When she kissed me, all lovey-dovey-like, right in front of them, Mom's face got red."

Dr. J jotted down some notes, but he didn't say a word.

"I sometimes wonder if my parents ever made love."

The doctor looked up from his notes with a questioning look.

"Mom's always telling me I was a 'miracle baby.' After two miscarriages, her doctor told her to stop trying. But she was convinced he was wrong and that she'd have a child."

"How did it feel when she called you a miracle?"

"I hated it. It was too much to handle, especially when I felt so inadequate. But Mom didn't stop with my birth. She was always telling me how amazingly smart and mature I was. 'You read by the time you were four. You skipped fifth grade. You learned the violin faster than any student Dr. Pillischer ever had.' She always told me how proud she was of me, and she'd pat my father on the hand and say, 'Dad's proud of you, too, aren't you, Frank?'"

Dr. J stared at me.

Remembering the question that started all this, I said, "So no, Doctor, Stephanie does not resemble my mother. Except for one thing. Both of them turned on me when the chips were down."

Dr. J gazed at me with those warm, understanding eyes of his that made me want to keep talking. But instead of responding to my comment, he glanced at his watch and told me our time was up.

As I drove home, I wondered why I'd said that Mother had let me down. Her loving concern had been my comfort during this horrific time. Then it came flooding back: the times in my childhood when she had given me the silent treatment if I did not obey her, just like Stephanie who refused to be honest, preferring silent distractions.

The next morning, anxiety awakened me, as usual. I trudged to the bedroom to take my pantheon of pills: Thorazine, Phenobarbital, prescription-strength antihistamine. As I swallowed them, my mind argued with itself.

What if I get hooked on all these medications?

Dr. J says that won't happen

What if he's wrong? I'll never get back into Hanover. And no woman will ever marry me.

Don't worry.

I can't stop worrying.

By midday I felt better. By the time I got to Dr. J's office the next day, I was ready to ask the question I'd saved until I had the courage to hear the answer: "Dr. Jacobson, how do you describe my illness?"

"You have anxiety neurosis."

His quick reply pierced right through my chest. I'd read about neuroses in my Abnormal Psychology course, though I couldn't remember much now. Internal thorns stabbed my stomach. "Am I ... abnormal?"

"A normal person is able to control his anxieties. But you're getting there. You're improving faster than most of my patients."

Where was the comfort in that?

3

January 5, 1955

"Thank you, Dr. J," I cried out when I ripped open the envelope my parents' mailman had just delivered and cried out, "Thank you!" I could not have earned the BA diploma I now held in my shaking hands if the good doctor hadn't arranged to transfer my credits from Hanover and set up a plan for me to finish my remaining thirteen credit hours at the University of Cincinnati. I had been able to graduate mid-term in Ohio.

I hurried to the kitchen and showed my degree to Mom and Dad, hugging them both. "Thanks for supporting me," I said, around the lump in my throat. They'd been my anchor, especially for the last three weeks. Following my breakdown, I'd managed to control my adrenaline, and it seemed my anxiety had crawled back into its cave.

After my mother found a frame for me, I took my prized possession to my bedroom at the end of the hall, to choose just the right spot to display it. But as I looked around, I was hit with the realization that I couldn't stay cocooned here forever. I needed to move on to whatever was next for me.

The big question was, what should I do with my life?

Back in high school, my church's youth leader and the pastor's wife had both encouraged me to think about becoming a pastor. At the time, the idea held no appeal for me whatsoever. But now I began to wonder if this was something I could do.

One cold evening, I curled up on the green sofa in my parents' living room to watch the movie *Hans Brinker, or the Silver Skates* on TV. I fantasized that I was Hans, crossing the finish line first against faster, stronger skaters. When I closed my eyes to savor the victory, a terrifying question ambushed me: Could someone who's lost it mentally ever stand tall in the pulpit?

I don't stand a chance . . . unless I guard the truth about my illness like a military secret.

Every day and night for a week, the question kept attacking me. Finally, an answer sneaked into my mind: Give it a try. I fought it off each time it slipped into my consciousness, which seemed like every minute. Then I recalled something my dad often said: "If you don't stick your neck out seventeen times a week, and get burned at least twice, you're not really living."

Dad was right. Really living means taking chances, even though you may get burned. I admired my father's determination and didn't want to let him down. But more important, I didn't want to let myself down. I was going to take a chance.

Wanting to know more about the ministry, I spent my days immersed in research. How many Presbyterian seminaries were there in the United States? Where were they located? What course of study would be required? That kept me busy, but I was still unsure where all this would lead.

One sunny day in early April, while heading for the kitchen to get breakfast, I saw the Cincinnati Presbytery newsletter lying on the hall table. I picked it up and saw an advertisement that seemed to be written just for me. "Interim pastor wanted for a five-church parish in Highland County for the summer. Modest salary. Part time or full time."

I picked up the phone and dialed, but stopped before punching in the last number. After writing down every word I wanted to say, I tapped the final digit. "Presbytery executive's office. This is Dr. Palmer."

I took a deep breath, then read my speech. "This is Bill Vamos. I'm calling in response to your ad for a pastor. Could you use a student who wants to try his wings before seminary?"

"Give me your phone number and I'll get back to you after I pray about it."

Dr. Palmer returned my call just two hours later. "When can you start?"

When could I start? How about yesterday! This was the second chance I yearned for. I knew there would be rough spots ahead, but at that moment I felt powerful enough to navigate whatever came my way.

At dinner that night, we celebrated. I had a job! Even if it was temporary. Mother made my favorite chicken-and-noodle dish. Dad let me do most of the talking, instead of his usual litany about his day. When we'd finished our chocolate-coconut cake with chocolate icing, Dad announced, "I'm proud of you, son. I know you're up to the job."

The light of the candles cast a soft glow on my mother's smiling face. A sense of confidence bubbled up inside me. I hadn't felt like this in a long time.

One month later, my parents and I left Cincinnati for Highland County in southern Ohio. The May countryside was alive with colorful redbuds, dogwood, and cherry blossoms. The plan was for them to help get me settled in the manse, my pastoral home for the next four months. We didn't talk much on the drive, enjoying the splendor around us. In Highland County, we turned off the main highway onto a gravel road. There at the end of the wide, dusty path stood a two-story gray manse. The dilapidated clapboard building looked like a relic from the past, but I couldn't wait to take a peek inside.

The downstairs living area, with its fireplace, bay window, and well-worn furniture, seemed to welcome me. A large desk dominated the small study. The window behind it overlooked the front yard, where a giant oak tree thrived.

I took the narrow stairs two at a time and found an attic bedroom with low-hanging beams. Perfect for a bachelor like me. Outside I noticed a tiny wooden structure with a moon-shaped hole in the door. It dawned on me that I hadn't seen a bathroom in the manse. I chuckled at the idea of using an outhouse. And I wondered what my parents would think of my living in a home without indoor plumbing.

After Dad and I emptied the car, Mom went to the kitchen to prepare supper from items she had brought with her. Dad and I went to the study. While I organized my desk, my father dusted the bookshelf. Without looking up, he said, "You know, Bill, there's a place for everything and everything in its place." Yes dad, I take your advice very seriously. When he looked up, he winked at me.

Mom called us to supper. As we ate bacon, lettuce, and tomato sandwiches, we talked about my future and what it would be like to serve five churches. I assured them I would be okay.

Once we polished off Mom's delicious chocolate-chip cookies, it was time for them to leave. Dad, stoic as ever, shook my hand and wished me the best. My mother gave me an extra-tight hug. I could tell she was trying hard not to cry.

When they were gone, the house felt empty. I felt empty too. My parents had been my "safe place" for the past year. Their departure left me with a terrible void.

I sprawled on the couch and spent a long time thinking and praying. And pondering what lay ahead for me.

But I couldn't lounge about for long. I had a sermon to write.

I was scheduled to preach to the Dellwood Presbyterian Church at 9:00 every other Sunday morning, alternating with the one in Grenville. Marshall was every other Sunday at 11:00 a.m., alternating with Mount Calvary. And Bethel at 2:00 p.m. every other week.

As I contemplated what I should say on my first Sunday as the pastor of five country churches in Highland County, Ohio, I thought of the great theologian Harry Emerson Fosdick, who preached in New York's Riverside Church and often moved America's prominent church men to tears. Of course, I knew nothing of biblical Hebrew and Greek, or even how to craft a sermon. But I was certain such formalities could wait until I started seminary in six months. Meanwhile, God and I would fill the pews of these five little churches.

When I preached in the 9:00 service at Dellwood, no one in the congregation moved an inch, so riveted were they by the sermon. Two older members fell asleep.

The fifteen-minute drive from Dellwood to Marshall took me forty-five minutes because I got lost. As I drove past one red barn after another, the rain and the deep brown earth told me God was there, but I began to doubt the existence of the Marshall Presbyterian Church. When I finally found the place, the attendance board on the gray wall next to the American flag showed a whopping twelve. Every single one of the dozen parishioners grabbed my hand like family members welcoming a long-lost cousin. "You're our first preacher in weeks."

After the service Lois Deachman invited me to dinner, but not before she commented about the sermon. "I think you will make it here; Uncle Desmond didn't fall asleep and you had interesting things to say". Then, at dinner, in a long-winded one-way conversation, she claimed most of the Marshall church members as her relatives. "Uncle Desmond always says, 'If the sermons are too heavy, we'll lose everybody. Pound your fist now and then, but mostly keep it light.' He's a part-time farmer and president of First National in Hillsboro. And my niece, Virginia, who's still single at forty-three, likes it quiet on Sunday mornings. She's all about inner peace. She says you ought to make lots of pastoral visits to the backsliders. Want another piece of rhubarb pie? You met my cousin Margaret this morning, another spinster. She says we need something to attract the kids. We haven't had any children in church for years."

While smiling attentively, I secretly planned a dazzling church program, certain to ignite all five churches with a spiritual bonfire. My sermons would mesmerize people, and the financial giving would increase exponentially. We'd have hay rides, wiener roasts, and some Saturday night dances to bring in the young people. I didn't know much about inner peace, though. I couldn't sit still when things were quiet. Perhaps a committee on prayer might do the job.

While Lois named every branch on her family tree, I mentally organized my schedule for the next few weeks. When I got my notes written down, I had so many reminders of committee meetings, hospitalized people, Sunday school teachers who needed to be replaced, requests to lead Bible studies, and countless other pushes and pulls, I felt more like a general trying to run five battalions than a member of a newly discovered church family.

After a month and a half, I learned that I had to work fifteen-hour days, seven days a week, to accomplish my mission.

The tranquilizers and antihistamines Dr. Jacobson had prescribed made my eyelids heavy. A visit to his office added another medication, an "upper" he called it, to keep me "balanced." At first, it made me feel as though caterpillars were crawling all over my body, but a lower dosage managed to calm me down.

Two months of preaching confirmed my love for the ministry. In spite of the long hours and unrealistic demands, I knew I wanted to go into preaching full time. I applied to Princeton Theological Seminary, believing it to be the top of the line. I waited anxiously for a reply.

When the response letter arrived, my pulse raced as I opened the envelope and read its contents. "We regret to inform you that your application for the 1955–56 school year has not been accepted. Princeton hears from so many promising students, such as yourself, but . . ."

I sank into the nearest chair, my heart aching.

In my next visit with Dr. J, he said, "Bill, you're one of the most intelligent patients I've ever had. Give another good seminary a chance to accept you."

But I was sure Hanover had blabbed about my breakdown when they sent my transcripts. Every seminary I apply will consider me too risky. Driving back to the manse after my appointment, I seriously considered resigning from the parish and moving back to my parents' house.

While planning my next sermon, I realized the people in my congregation hungered for spiritual food, and it was my job to feed them. I couldn't let them down just because I had some personal garbage to deal with. Besides, it went against my nature to give up.

That Sunday, I presented a fiery sermon to the folks at the Marshall church. Even the usual sleepers were wide awake. Afterward, as I greeted parishioners at the door, many told me how much they appreciated me. "Your sincerity touches my heart," one woman gushed. "Someday you'll move on to a bigger church than ours. And they'll be lucky to get you." I deeply appreciated her comment. It seemed to be confirmation that I had made the right decision not to quit.

My service at the Grenville church went much the same way. But when I arrived at Bethel Presbyterian at two in the afternoon for my third performance of the day, attendance was a grand total of one. I preached my carefully constructed sermon anyway.

I didn't know Sam Baker well, but I'd liked him from our first handshake. If he was embarrassed by being the only one in attendance, he hid it well. He listened carefully to each point in the sermon, smiled at my jokes, and nodded with approval when I struck a chord with which he resonated. After the service, he shook my hand, congratulated me on a "fine" sermon, and said it was a shame more folks weren't there to hear it. Then he scurried out the sanctuary door, muttering something about it being time to milk the cows.

The following Sunday, I repeated my speech to my Dellwood church, with much the same results. This time, fifteen people showed up. Everyone assured me that was a good Sunday's attendance.

At Mount Calvary, the largest of my five churches, a special program had been planned by the County Grange Rural Fraternity in place of the worship service for that Sunday. I was to give the opening prayer, but nothing more. This congregation would have to hear my powerful sermon some other time.

When I arrived at the church, I joined a standing-room-only crowd. As I searched for a seat in the packed auditorium, Betty Smithers, a petite woman with brown eyes, pulled me aside. "There's a chair reserved for you in the front row. Your message will be the last one in the program."

Message? So much for only doing the opening prayer.

Although the room was filled with noisy gabbing, all I could hear was the sledgehammer pounding inside my head. My fiery sermon didn't seem appropriate to end a special event like this. But I hadn't prepared anything else.

I sat in that front row, trying to compose myself, unaware of anything around me. *This is the stuff that nightmares are made of.*

I remembered a sermon I had preached for Youth Sunday when I was in high school. The people in this congregation had never heard it. Though I'd given it a long time ago, I still remembered most of it. And there were parts of the speech that seemed especially appropriate for this event.

I tried to appear calm, but my insides felt raw from anxiety. *Lord, just get me through this.*

When my turn came, I took my place at the podium and looked out at the crowd. Much to my surprise, when I began to speak, a sense of calm settled over me, and I realized I could do this. The further I got into my talk, the more confident I felt. Even in that crowded room, you could have heard an ant making its way across the well-worn oak floor.

I ended with a rousing flourish. God had come through . . . with a little help from me.

As people walked out, they shook my hand and complimented me on my "outstanding sermon."

"You must have worked long and hard on that," one parishioner chirped.

If he only knew!

When I returned to the parsonage, I collapsed on the recliner in my study. I rested my head against the worn leather and picked up my pipe from the end table. The smoke relaxed my tired mind, bringing new thoughts, followed by prayer.

It still hurt that I'd been rejected by Princeton. I was thankful that even my old sermon had spoken to God's people. It confirmed that I actually could preach. But I questioned my calling. After all, I still needed to learn the fundamentals of preaching.

Maybe I should give up the ministry.
I can't do that.
But what if no seminary will accept me?
How will I know if I don't give it a try?

4

A week after delivering my powerful prepared sermon, I applied to McCormick Theological Seminary in Chicago. When I received the letter of acceptance, I dropped into my swivel chair and circled around and around, congratulating myself. Then I called my folks, who responded with excitement.

After hanging up, I sat in the quiet of my study, daydreaming about the future, which looked bright and hopeful. But, as in a dream, I awakened to the reality of having to leave these wonderful folks I had come to care about. I'd only been hired for the summer, and my four months were nearly over. On the following Sunday I reminded each church that I would be leaving in a few weeks. Even though most of the congregations knew I would be attending seminary in the fall, it still caught many off guard.

That last month, I worked hard to prepare my churches for the future. Several of the families thanked me for my service by inviting me into their homes for a meal.

I took great pains writing my farewell sermon, but preaching it was even harder. "Today is the last Sunday I will be in your pulpit," I said to the folks at Belfast. I stopped and looked down, struggling to keep my composure. "I want to thank you for what you've done for me: encouraging me, loving me, and overlooking my shortcomings. It is because of you that I have decided to go into the ministry full time."

Looking around, I saw many long faces. *God, they will never know how much they have helped to heal this battered human.*

After the service there was an outpouring of hugs and well wishes.

"We'll miss you, Bill."

"We hate to see you leave us, but we're glad you're going to seminary."

Lois Deachman, with hands on her hips and a twinkle in her eyes, strolled over to where I stood. "The church has started to grow, and our young people are coming to church, people are listening to your sermons, and you're leaving us?" She smiled and gave me a big hug.

The leaves of autumn were just beginning to lay their colorful carpet over the countryside when I left my Highland County Parish and headed for Illinois.

McCormick Seminary did not disappoint. I sat under the tutelage of the top theological scholars of the time. At the end of the first semester, I took a killer of a Church History class. The second-year seminary students had warned me that it would be the most difficult class I would take and that very few students made above a C+ on the final exam.

They were right. The test contained a breadth of questions that made me certain I would fail. But I tried my hardest and hoped for the best.

When I finally escaped the classroom, I headed for the campus post office, hoping for a letter from my parents. Instead I found a letter from Dr. Palmer, saying, "The churches of Highland County Parish want you back for next summer." I leaped into the air, my books flying everywhere. Everyone on campus must have heard my loud "Yippee!" I couldn't wait to get back to where I felt needed and valued.

When I called Dr. Palmer to accept, he asked if I would be interested in attending a week-long training session for Vacation Bible School teachers that would start in early June. "The event will be held at Camp Presmont in southeastern Ohio."

My mind traveled back to the previous summer, when I took some of Mount Calvary's young people to Camp Presmont for a day trip. The facility was surrounded on all sides by a thick green forest. Nestled among the oak, pine, and dogwood trees lay beautiful Lake Presmont, where young campers canoed along the shore, trying to avoid the campers who were learning to swim. One large building housed the dining hall and some classrooms. Wood-chip trails led to cabins and tents scattered throughout the woods. All the paths converged on an outdoor worship area with plank benches that formed a semicircle, facing a large wooden cross.

Eager to visit Camp Presmont again, and grateful for a chance to meet new people and make friends, I accepted Dr. Palmer's invitation.

I wondered if there was any chance that I'd meet someone special at camp. Feeling ready to think about settling down and starting a family, I took out a blank sheet of paper, grabbed a pen, and jotted down the traits I wanted to find in a wife. After wasting far too much time on this project, I read through my list. *Why would any woman who had all of these wonderful qualities be interested in me?*

I needed to stop daydreaming and get back to work. I crumpled up the paper, flung it across the desk, and forced myself to focus on preparation of my next sermon.

I arrived at the VBS training center just in time for lunch. The moment I entered the dining hall, I noticed a lovely young woman with light-brown, shoulder-length hair with bangs, wearing a red-

and-white polka-dot dress. She radiated a wholesomeness that my parents would definitely approve of.

Her blue eyes brightened as I approached her. I glanced at her name tag, which had "JO" written in bold letters. But before I could introduce myself, a male voice interrupted. "Hey, Bill! Do you remember me?"

I didn't see Jo again until the afternoon swim at the lake.

As she walked toward the diving board in a black one-piece bathing suit, I couldn't help but notice how sexy she looked, even though I knew I shouldn't be thinking that way. But she caught my eye the way a beautiful painting makes a person stop and stare.

She stood on the board for a moment, the sun glistening on the lake around her. After adjusting her bathing cap, she dove into the cerulean water. Emerging from the lake, she picked up her towel and walked over to a group of gals, probably her roommates.

At supper, she was again surrounded by friends. Would I ever get a chance to talk to this woman alone?

Early the next morning, the clanging of the old farm bell jarred me awake. The smell of musty mildew, which permeated the walls of the log cabin, assaulted me. But outside, the purple-red sky of the sunrise was a promise of a beautiful day. And the intoxicating smell of frying bacon pulled sleepy conferees like me straight toward the dining room.

After breakfast, the hard work of learning to be Vacation Bible School teachers began. The conference directors divided the attendees into groups of ten. To my disappointment, Jo wasn't in my small group. I assumed that meant I would see her only at meals and closing worship.

Class time was spent learning new songs, studying Bible passages, and role-playing how to teach VBS. Throughout the afternoon, I tried to meet Jo. But I only managed a few seconds of eye contact with this captivating woman, when she passed me on her way to the lake.

That evening, I saw her in a yellow canoe, seated next to a homely-looking guy who was lucky enough to be in her small group. She smiled at me. Blood rushed to my sunburned face. At least I had caught her attention.

Throughout the rest of the conference, each small group hung together. None of the women in my group took my eye like the gal in the red-and-white polka-dot dress.

On the last night of training, we all sat around the campfire for worship. I caught Jo looking at me. When I smiled, she smiled back, then lowered her head as if embarrassed. She didn't look at me again during the rest of the service. But I felt we had made a connection.

The next morning, I rushed to the dining room, where the summer assignments were posted. I scanned the list carefully. My heart sank when I found that Jo was not assigned to teach VBS at my parish in Highland County, Ohio. Instead she would be teaching in Youngstown, Ohio—with the homely-looking guy.

I drove home from the conference determined to forget this entrancing woman and focus instead on the five churches I was privileged to serve again.

As I was preparing a sermon, the telephone screamed its usual off-key interruption. I jumped as I grabbed for the receiver.

"Bill Vamos, Charles Muller here. I'm with the Muller, Stark, Mitchell Funeral Home. One of your members expired this morning. Sara Hankins, ninety-seven years old, heart failure. You've never met her, but this lady was special. She spent her life praying for and helping others. She deserves the best we can give her."

I'd never conducted a funeral. I didn't even have any training yet. I called Dr. Deakler in Lakeside. He had thirty-five years of experience in parish ministry. He gave me some great suggestions.

Three days later, at 12:30 p.m., I pulled my '53 Ford station wagon into the parking lot. As I opened my car door, Charles Muller grabbed my arm and hustled me to a highly polished black Cadillac. "We have just thirty minutes to get to the Dellwood Church," he announced. "Sorry to make you come here first, but there's some last-minute information I have to tell you."

Muller opened the passenger door for me, I skipped around to the other side, and climbed into the Cadillac. His steely green eyes almost pierced through the steering column as he started the engine.

The car's movement soothed my prickly nerves. I actually began to look forward to the funeral service. I had prepared well and had generated a friendly rapport with the family. I laid my neck on the seatback. Thoughts of Jo swept over my brain.

Muller's voice interrupted my musings. "I need to fill you in on some traditions we keep in these parts. Now, about the opening of the service . . ."

I resisted the funeral director's pushy attitude. It was nicer to keep thinking about Jo. I caught isolated blurbs from Muller's lecture.

"In the Dellwood Church, we always close the casket before the pastor leads the service. Been doing it that way for fifty years."

I wondered how a guy like me could catch a firefly like Jo. From what I had seen of her, she appeared to be confident, warm, spontaneous, whereas I always organized everything ahead of time, to make sure nothing went wrong. I thought about the made-to-order wife sheet I'd come up with. *I make too many lists.*

"The people never stand during a funeral." Muller rapped on the steering wheel to emphasize his point. "You stand to lead the service, but the people are always sitting."

Jo is so vivacious. If I were to paint her portrait, I would need all the colors of the rainbow!

As the Cadillac turned into the Dellwood Church driveway, I tried to recall Muller's messages. Did he say to close the casket at the beginning or the end? One thing I knew for sure: the people stood throughout the service. Or did they?

I got out of the Cadillac, climbed the familiar steps, and unlocked the church door.

The Dellwood folks viewed their one-room church as a rare architectural gem. The tower stretched skyward from a sharply peaked roof, which seemed as if it prayed for people all week long. I always felt connected when I walked into that building. The polished oak pulpit rose from the center of the chancel, solid and strong. The old-fashioned pews and patched red carpeting whispered, *Welcome home, friend.*

Promptly at 1:30, the organist played "Faith of Our Fathers." My nervous system was like a twisted tightrope. I had decided how to handle the standing-sitting and open-or-closed casket questions. I hoped I had those things right.

When the organist stopped, I took a giant step into the pulpit and asked the people to stand for the call to worship and invocation. Charles Muller scurried down the aisle, folded in the linens and pillow and closed the casket, then did a quick turnaround. He almost tripped as he returned, scowling, to the back of the sanctuary.

My colossal mistake shadowed my conscience all the way to the graveside. As I led the short service, trying to make eye contact with the grieving people, one flap of the drooping burial tent billowed at the back of my head. I braced myself for a storm of protests.

Marshall Denton was Dellwood's most influential church member. "Reverend," he said, as people began to leave the grave site. "I want to thank you from the bottom of my heart. The way you had us stand in the beginning, with her casket open—what a tribute to such a special woman!"

"Thank you," I exhaled, still struggling to stop the merry-go-round whirling inside me.

Marshall Denton moved on to shake hands with Charles Muller. "You used such wisdom in advising our young preacher to break with tradition just this once. You're not afraid to step out on a limb now and then. I like that, Charles."

When I returned to the manse, I shuffled to my desk and sank into the wheeled chair. Through the sun-washed windows on one side of my modest study, I watched two crows land on top of the shed in the backyard. They harmonized beautifully as they performed their minor-key song.

As I inhaled a lungful of air in an attempt to settle myself, I noticed a crumpled-up note on the corner of my desktop. I opened it and read the words I'd hastily scribbled down the day Dr. Palmer invited me to attend the VBS camp:

What to Look for in a Wife

1. Must be gorgeous, outgoing, charming, and humble.
2. Must be intelligent and perceptive, with a twinkle in her eyes.
3. Must play the piano, type 100 words per minute, and cook enviable meals.
4. Must keep a tidy, spotless house, be well organized, and be serious about life.
5. Must have a spontaneous sense of humor.

I pictured Jo's thick brown hair tied back in a ponytail and wondered if she could type, cook, or sing. She was certainly bubbly, outgoing, and confident. But I didn't know her well enough to gauge her humility. I put a question mark next to the word *humble*.

Determined to stop daydreaming, I threw the list into the wastebasket and immersed myself in writing my sermon for the week. As I reached for a book of sermon illustrations, my elbow brushed against a pile of papers on my desk, exposing a memo I'd typed a week ago, which said, "June 1: Bale hay for Elee." June 1 was the next day!

I had made a deal with Elee Copher, a local farmer, when I'd called on him at home. I agreed to work for him on Saturday, and, in exchange, he'd come to church that Sunday. Elee probably thought he was leading a lamb to the slaughter. But I was young and physically fit, so I didn't figure I'd have any trouble lifting a few bales of hay.

Still, I'd need a good night's sleep, so I headed straight to bed.

I arrived at Elee's farm promptly at six the next morning. I leaped enthusiastically onto one of the sagging hay-baling wagons, joining seven other hired men who leaned against the wooden sides, each holding a foam cup of coffee. They nodded politely as I found a place to hang on. As the wagon bounced across the field, nobody spoke, everyone seemingly lost in his own world.

The rain of the night before had left a fine mist on the bales of hay, making them heavier. For two hours, I stumbled over the clumpy field, lifting and heaving the huge, scratchy bales. When I couldn't lift any more, Elee sent me to the barn, where every summer allergy I had ever experienced kicked in. My eyes watered, my nose ran, I couldn't stop sneezing. Finally, after a half hour of torture, Elee took pity on me and redirected me to a wagon back in the field. The other two guys there pitched bales faster than I could catch them, and several of my bales fell off the wagon.

Lunchtime felt like a desert oasis. As I fought to keep my eyes open while I shoveled fried chicken, mashed potatoes, green beans, and rhubarb cobbler into my mouth, I wondered where we would all go for an afternoon snooze. But as soon as we'd cleared our plates, Elee marched us back outside.

All afternoon, I hoisted, itched, snorted, and prayed for more rain under the clear blue sky. I could hardly wait for sundown.

When I finally crawled into bed that night, I was covered with sweat, scratches, and sunburn.

But true to his word, Elee came to church the next day. I smiled when I spotted him slumped in an aisle seat of the balcony's last row.

Unfortunately, that was the only time I ever saw him in church. But part of me was relieved that he didn't offer the same bargain again. I had no desire to return to that farm. Ever!

Chapter Two

Jo

1

THE SUMMER I FINISHED MY FRESHMAN YEAR at Berea College in Kentucky, I wanted to do something different—something for the world and for God.

A few summers before, when I was fourteen, I had worked in New York State as a chambermaid for the Lutheran House at the Chautauqua Institution. It was a beautiful resort, with a lake surrounded by quaint historic homes, and a center for the cultural arts. The pay wasn't wonderful, but the hours were flexible, and I enjoyed the people. Chautauqua also had lots of interesting college boys.

In the summers that followed, I'd worked in a bookstore, as an usher for the opera, and at the refectory, where I was allowed to eat as much ice cream as I wanted. That was great, until a day came when I didn't want to even see another ice cream cone perhaps for the rest of my life.

One of my most interesting jobs was walking a blind lady through the plaza. She was a bit brittle, and very critical of her family because she believed they just wanted her money. As we walked, I described the people passing by and anything I thought might interest her. When we finished our walk, I read to her from the morning newspaper.

I could have returned to any of these jobs. But this summer I was ready for a new experience.

As I contemplated my options, my sister Lois told me there was a job opening in southern Ohio, teaching Vacation Church School. This sounded exciting, so I applied and was accepted—provided I went through training in late May, which I did happily.

The day I left, Lois called. "Maybe this summer you'll meet the man you're going to marry," she teased, aware that there would be young seminarians at the training session. Our family was rich with Presbyterian pastors. My grandfather, father, brother, brother-in-law, and her husband were all ordained ministers.

"I'm only nineteen," I argued.

"I realize that." She chuckled. "But you never know."

The pale greens of spring had just begun to deepen when I arrived at Camp Presmont near Cincinnati. I headed straight to the lodge, which was abuzz with college people waiting to register.

The girl at the registration desk informed me that the first training session would begin after lunch. Once I'd finished registering, I hurried to the girls' cabins, east of the lodge. A loud chorus of voices welcomed me to cabin four. As the last one to arrive, I threw my suitcase on the only empty upper bunk.

My seven roommates and I made quick introductions, then headed for the dining room. Everyone there seemed to be talking at once. The tin roof intensified the babble of voices. The eight of us found a round table close to the buffet, and we took our seats. Before long, our table was called to the food line. I was too excited to be hungry, so I took only some salad and a chocolate brownie.

Back at the table, the conversation centered on expectations of the conference, where we lived, where we'd gone to school, and where we grew up. When I said that I'd been raised in Cameroon, West Africa, where my parents were Presbyterian missionaries, the girl next to me nearly dropped her fork full of pasta. "Really?" Her blue-green eyes sparkled through her glasses. "What was that like?"

"It was fun. Except for the year I was in third grade and had to go to boarding school. I got really homesick for my mother."

As the other girls talked about their backgrounds, I occasionally glanced around the dining room to see if any interesting-looking young guys might be at the conference. To my disappointment, no one caught my eye.

Just as I finished my last bite of brownie, the double doors of the dining room flew open and a young man bounded in. Everyone in the room seemed to stop and stare.

"Hi, Bill," a male voice called out.

"Hey, Jim!" He crossed the room with confidence, his brown eyes smiling behind dark-framed glasses, his crew cut perfectly combed. He passed my table on his way to talk to his friend.

Something about Bill fascinated me. Throughout the training sessions, I tried to get to know him better. But I never had much of an opportunity to talk with him.

On the last week of the session, I started hoping I might be sent to work at one of his churches in Highland County Parish. But neither of my summer assignments was at any of his churches. When training ended, I thought I would never see him again.

But after my initial assignment to a church in Youngstown, Ohio, I was assigned to teach Vacation Bible School at a church in Southern Ohio for two weeks. My heart leapt. I was going to get my wish of getting to know Bill Vamos after all.

A bus took me to Highland County one windy Saturday in August. When it approached the designated parking stall, I wondered if anyone would be there to meet me. I looked out the window and saw Bill, pacing like a pent-up tiger. My heart skipped a beat.

When I stepped off the bus, he welcomed me warmly and took my suitcase. He ushered me to his Ford station wagon in the parking lot. "You'll be staying at Mrs. Slade's house. She's a widow with a great sense of humor, and she's gentle with people. You'll like her, I'm sure."

"I'm anxious to meet her. Is she one of your church members?"

"Yes. She attends the Grenville Church, where your Vacation Bible School will be held."

"Great! I'm really looking forward to meeting her. It will be quite a change teaching in a rural area. My first assignment was in the inner city."

"This will definitely be different." He smiled at me. "But I know my church members will love you."

My cheeks warmed as I thanked him for his gracious comment. Twenty minutes later, we turned onto Third Street. As the Ford rolled onto the driveway, a tall, stocky woman was on the porch, waiting for us, a colorful apron tied around her plump waist, and tightly curled salt-and-pepper hair encircling her joyful face.

I stepped out of the car, and as I reached for her hand, she threw her arms around me. "Welcome! I'm Mrs. Slade. I'm so glad you're here." When the formal introductions were over, she asked Bill, "Would you please take Jo's suitcase upstairs to the bedroom on the right?"

After Bill left with my luggage, Mrs. Slade offered to get me a cup of tea or a glass of water. When I assured her I was fine, she led me to the living room, which was filled with antique furniture. She directed me to sit on a love seat covered with blue velvet. As soon as she sat beside me, I started asking questions about the Vacation Bible School, which would start the following Monday. Her answers made me feel comfortable and confident.

When Bill returned, Mrs. Slade excused herself and headed to the kitchen. He sat in an upholstered chair opposite me, and I asked if there was anything he wanted me to know about his church.

"Service starts at nine a.m. tomorrow."

I chuckled at his matter-of-fact answer. "Is there anything I should know about the people in your congregation?"

He crossed his arms and leaned back in his chair. "Don't take them too seriously. There are a few pieces of sandpaper in the Grenville Church, but I'm sure you can handle them. Just be yourself."

"I'll certainly try." I felt silly about telling him that I'd *try* to be myself. But I didn't let on how foolish I felt.

After we talked awhile, Bill glanced at his watch. "I have to be on my way." He jumped up from his chair walked to the doorway, then turned, a boyish grin on his face. "But I'll see you tomorrow," he said, and winked at me.

"Won't you join us for dinner, Bill?" Mrs. Slade called from the kitchen.

"Thanks, but I have an appointment." He waved at both of us, then walked out the door.

As I helped Mrs. Slade prepare sandwiches and fruit for the evening meal, I thought about how confident Bill seemed in my abilities and how comfortable I felt around him. I was excited about spending two weeks getting to know him better.

The birdsong outside my bedroom window awakened me early the next morning. I put on a plain white cotton blouse and a red print skirt with white flowers that hugged my waist and flared as it moved down past my knees. It felt comfortably conservative—just right to be wearing for the Grenville folks, I figured.

After breakfast, I walked to the church, arriving there a few minutes before nine. Organ music played as I entered the half-filled sanctuary. The building smelled musty and old, but the burgundy carpet and the well-worn communion table welcomed me. I took a seat in the second row from the front.

Bill sat on an old high-backed pine chair a few feet behind the pulpit, his head bowed. Praying, no doubt. When the music stopped, he stood, gripped the sides of the pulpit, and leaned forward, making eye contact with each of his parishioners. When he saw me, he focused on my face, which turned hot. I looked down, wondering if anyone had noticed the flush in my cheeks.

I also wondered if Bill felt as uneasy as I did.

When he began preaching, I sensed a bit of nervousness in Bill as he stumbled over a few words. But he soon relaxed, which gave me permission to enjoy the sermon. And the attractive young pastor.

His tall, slim body looked handsome in a navy-blue suit, white shirt, and blue-and-white polka-dot tie. His brown eyes shone as he delivered his three-point sermon. I was amazed at how well he preached. *What is it about this man that is so appealing?* He seemed . . . innocent. Unspoiled.

At the end of the service, a pretty young woman ran up to me. "I'm Natalie Cummins. Would you like to see where Vacation Bible School will be held?" Before I could answer, she grabbed my hand and led me down a narrow stairway.

The basement was brilliantly lit with fluorescent ceiling lights reflecting white walls, covered with brightly painted children's art. The large room was partitioned into three separate areas, each covered with a colorful rug, giving the area a warm cheerfulness.

"The kids must love it here," I said.

Her face brightened. "I hope so. We've tried to make it a happy place."

We walked back upstairs and found Bill talking to a church elder, who ducked out the door when he saw us. Natalie chatted for a while, then excused herself, leaving Bill and me alone.

"You did a beautiful job with your sermon this morning. You seem to enjoy preaching."

"I do. It's my favorite part of the week."

As we continued to talk, Bill put his hands in his pockets and stared at his feet, as if steeling himself for something. Finally, he asked, "Would you go swimming with me tomorrow night?"

I smiled. "I'd love to."

He stepped back and mumbled, "Oh," as if stunned that I accepted his invitation so quickly.

Bill and I arrived at Rocky Four Lake, outside of Hillsboro, Ohio, in the late evening. The night air was warm and the full moon reflected silver rays on the water's surface, making it a perfect night for a swim. But in all the excitement, I had forgotten to bring my bathing suit.

Great way to make a good impression!

When I told Bill, he laughed. I laughed too. Instead of swimming, we placed our towels on the sand and identified constellations: the Big Dipper, the Little Dipper, Orion. It was a good way to break the ice. But I wanted to talk about our lives.

I had never been shy about asking people questions in order to get to know them better. So, after chatting for a while, I asked something I figured he would be comfortable answering. "Why do you want to be a pastor?"

He took a deep breath. "My mother was a Christian Scientist and my father a Roman Catholic. When I was in junior high, my parents joined a Methodist Church, hoping to present a united front that would guide me into faith. But the pastor shouted, fumed, and pounded his fists on the pulpit, trying to frighten his people into heaven. At least that's how it seemed to me."

My hands flew to my mouth. "It's hard to believe that anyone would listen to a pastor with that kind of preaching."

"In the middle of my sophomore year of high school, we moved from Pittsburg to Terre Haute, Indiana. The day we arrived a scholarly looking kid introduced himself as John Weberg. He offered to introduce me to some neighborhood kids my age." Bill dug his toes into the sand. "John invited me to their youth group. Even though I felt scared, I went. When I walked into the meeting room in the basement of the church, my hands were shaking and my mouth was dry. John introduced me to a dozen strangers, who were sitting in a circle on dark brown metal chairs, each one holding a Bible. A fair-skinned, curly-haired guy greeted me with a smile that melted some of my fear. He offered to let me sit by him."

I felt honored that he was sharing such an important event in his life, and in such detail.

"Those young people started discussing creation, and the leader asked me to chime in anytime, as though he thought I might have something worthwhile to say. I just fought to stay in my chair and resist scrambling up the steps and go screaming out the door."

"Why did you feel that way?"

"At that point in my life I felt like I was nothing. Like I didn't belong there, I wasn't good enough."

It was hard to understand how this sensitive but confident young man sitting next to me on the sand could have felt so unworthy. I wanted to know why, but I decided to wait. It was too soon in our relationship to ask him such a personal question.

"When it was time for prayer, the gal next to me whispered, 'You can pray silently if you want.' So, I sat up straight and squeezed my eyelids shut and waited for someone to say amen. When I heard that magic word, I bolted out of there."

"Did you ever go back?"

"I returned every week for two years, because I found something there that had eluded me everywhere else. My visits with this group were like an island oasis, where friendly natives kept pulling me to shore. When my words froze in my throat, they waited until I recovered, and they continued to listen as long as I wanted to talk. When I brought up controversial topics, the group exploded into a verbal free-for-all, and no one was upset. Instead they praised me for letting them argue. They accepted me. That's when I decided there was something special about this Christian thing, and I wanted to be a part of it."

I placed my hand on his shoulder. "That youth group changed your life, didn't it?"

"Yes, it did."

"Was that when you decided to be a pastor?"

"It was certainly the spark that lit a fire under me, which led me in the direction of the pastorate."

I'd dated lots of guys, but none of them had ever been as vulnerable with me as Bill. He was willing to share the deep pieces of himself, and I valued that in him.

Every night after that, we took long walks over country roads lit by the moon reflecting its light on our path. The loosely packed dirt felt cool, sifting through our toes as we strolled up and down South Street, sharing openly about our lives.

On one such night, Bill offered to show me one of the other churches he was serving. We returned to his car and headed for Dellwood, three miles away.

External floodlights bathed the church's white frame exterior in brilliant light. The building looked like a painting, dwarfed by the darkness surrounding it.

When Bill pulled into the parking lot, I noticed a freshly painted outhouse. Since I'd lived in Africa for six years, the tiny wooden building seemed a natural part of the landscape.

As we entered the sanctuary, it became evident to me that this one-room church was part of history. The red carpet was very worn. A battered upright piano stood near a raised area that must have served as the choir loft. Even the musty smells conveyed the message *I have been here for a long time.*

I gazed at the stained-glass window behind the pulpit, which portrayed scenes from the life of Christ. I felt at peace just looking at it.

As we stood among the dusty pews, Bill leaned toward me and kissed me. His lips were tender. I pulled him close and kissed him back.

I looked forward to our nightly walks, holding hands and kissing often. On the nights when the heavens released their raindrops, we took refuge in the Dellwood Church.

One night, as we sat on the well-worn wooden pews, Bill asked, "Do you remember meeting Myra Simpson?"

"Is she the one who wears her salt-and-pepper hair in a bun on top of her head?"

He grinned. "That's her. Well, Myra invited me to dinner last Sunday for her famous mouth-watering fried chicken. I ate enough food to last me for a week. But after I finished eating, I excused myself and headed for Sue Hankin's house to eat again."

I chuckled, thinking that pastors must get awfully fat if they accepted every meal invitation they received from their congregations. Surely, he could have at least spread out his acceptances a bit. "Why did you eat two big meals in one day?"

He looked at me sheepishly. "Because I knew you'd be there."

I couldn't help but smile, feeling warm inside.

Bill continued, "Sue Hankin's mission in life seems to be to stuff her friends."

I recalled the spread she'd put out the previous Sunday. Homemade rolls, both sweet potatoes and mashed, green beans, tomatoes, cucumbers, lettuce, seven-bean and fruit salads, chicken and dressing, ham, roast beef, apple pie, and ice cream. The entire congregation could have eaten for a week on the food she served the two of us.

Bill continued, "When I finished dinner that night, I hurt so much I couldn't move. I just sat there trying to flex my sloshing stomach muscles. And I thought how crazy it was for me to let you drive me to the brink of a gastric disaster. No matter how charming and irresistible you are."

We both exploded in laughter.

He thinks I'm charming and irresistible! I wondered where this relationship would lead.

At the end of my two-week VBS, Bill and I both knew we wanted our relationship to continue. But I had to return to Berea College in Kentucky for my sophomore year, and Bill needed to take his middle year at McCormick Seminary in Chicago. Before we left for our respective schools, we resolved to write each other at least once a week, and Bill promised to try to come to Berea every month for a visit.

Mother had rented a small upstairs apartment at Berea, where my sister Ruth and I also stayed. Mother's real home was in Cameroon, West Africa, doing mission work. But she had decided to spend her one-year furlough with us at Berea.

During one of Bill's monthly visits, Mother and Ruth went shopping, leaving us alone. We held each other, stealing kisses. Suddenly Bill whispered, "There's something I need to tell you." He reached for my hand. I saw a sadness in his face, as if he were about to reveal something deep and painful. "I hope you won't think any less of me after you hear this."

"Okay," I replied softly, trying to appear brave.

"Two years ago, when I was a junior in college . . ." He took a deep breath, staring at the gray carpet. "I—I had a breakdown."

I wondered what kind of a breakdown he was talking about.

"When I was a child, one of my mother's friends experienced a mental breakdown. I was too young to comprehend what that meant, but I knew something was very wrong with her." He wrung his hands. "A few years ago, I started experiencing some of the same symptoms as my mom's friend."

I waited for Bill to explain. After what seemed a long time, he raised his head and his eyes searched my face. He looked like a lost bear cub hoping to be found before he fell into a cave. I scooted closer to him. "Can you tell me more?"

"It started when I couldn't sleep. And my thoughts kept getting all tangled up. My mind became irrational, torturous. I tried to keep others from knowing. But my fraternity brothers saw my pain, and one of them took me to my parents' home."

My stomach tightened as I braced myself for what he was about to tell me.

"I had to be hospitalized for two months. It was hell. But when I finally got out, the doctors said that these symptoms would never happen to me again." Bill wiped his tear-streaked cheeks, then looked me in the eye. "I promise you, Jo, I will never have to be hospitalized for mental issues again."

He broke into sobs, and I held him close. "It's all right. I love you no matter what." I didn't know what the future might hold. But I knew I was in love with this gentle man of incredible faith.

When he had composed himself, I asked him about his stay in the hospital and about school at McCormick. We talked until the sun disappeared and street lights cast shadows through the living-room windows. During a pause in our conversation, Bill reached into his pocket and pulled out a small box. I knew what would be in it. We had talked about marriage many times. He opened the box, revealing a diamond ring. He put it on my finger. "Will you marry me Jo?"

"Yes, Bill, I will," thinking about nothing but my love for this amazing man.

Two weeks after we were engaged, my mother suggested I consider spending my junior year of college abroad. She liked Bill, but she had heard from the wife of the president of Hanover College that Bill had had a serious breakdown in his junior year. Mother was worried. I suspected she hoped that the year abroad would break up my relationship with Bill.

Confident that nothing could stop us from being married if it was God's will, I applied to the Board of Foreign Missions and was one of fifty students chosen to spend my junior year of college studying abroad. The board assigned me to India.

I was excited about the prospect of studying in another country. But I wondered how Bill would take the news. Would he encourage me to go, recognizing it as a once-in-a-lifetime opportunity? Or would he beg me not to go, concerned about how the long separation would affect our relationship?

Knowing this wouldn't be an easy conversation, I wrote down everything I wanted to say. When he picked up the phone, I almost decided the timing was wrong. But after taking a deep breath, I blurted out, "I have a chance to spend my junior year studying at Isabella Thoburn College in India."

After a long pause, Bill congratulated me, then asked questions, like how long I'd be gone, what the college was like, where it was.

"I can understand why you're excited," he said. "I won't stand in your way."

Would I have forgone the trip if Bill had objected? I'm not sure. But his gracious encouragement relieved the pressure. I was impressed with his integrity, and his maturity.

2

Stifling heat hung in the motionless air the week of June 17, 1957. Along with four other American girls, I boarded a plane for the first leg of our three-week trip to India.

Our first stop was New York City, where for seven days the Board of Missions prepared us to meet the demands of a year abroad. Our tireless work left little time to enjoy the sights. As the week wore on, we gave in to fatigue. But we were ready for our trip.

Around noon we boarded an Italian ship, *Giulio Cesare*, headed for Italy. The week-long voyage was spent eating, swimming, reading, having devotions on deck, and more eating.

One starry night, as romantic Italian music played throughout the ship and loving couples strolled the deck, I grabbed some stationery, settled into a lounge chair, and composed a letter to Bill.

"I think I may die of longing for you," I wrote. But the anticipation of reaching India took the edge off my yearning heart.

My friends and I were well rested when we arrived in Rome. I found the city electrifying, with a multiplicity of intriguing sights. Because our hotel was near the downtown area, we walked to the Coliseum, the Pantheon, and many museums. We tossed coins into the Trevi Fountain. I fell in love with Michelangelo's *Pietà* at St. Peter's Basilica. One evening, sitting among the ancient ruins, we watched the opera *Tosca* by Puccini. I knew I would never be able to fully recapture the beauty of that evening, but I was equally certain the memory would linger on.

Wherever we went, people stared at the five of us. Was it because we were Americans? Or because we were vivacious, attractive college girls? Maybe both. Being whistled at and occasionally patted on the bottom was flattering. But because we were Americans, the merchants all thought we had money, so they raised their prices. After a while, it became tiresome. On our way to the airport on our last day in Italy, the taxi driver overcharged us. That was the last straw.

"We're not paying that," I shouted, wagging my finger at him. "We are poor American students." The other girls chimed in, and he finally relented and lowered his asking price.

Our next flight took us to Beirut, where we had one day to see the sights before our next connection. After the hustle and bustle of New York and Rome, Beirut was a welcome relief. Our hotel was right on the ocean, and it looked like something that could grace the cover of a travel magazine.

As soon as I unpacked, I changed into a swimsuit and headed for a lounge chair by the pool. I gazed out at the ocean, the water sparkling like lacework, reflecting the brilliant blue sky. I looked toward the horizon, aching at the great distance that separated me from Bill. Yet thoughts of him were muted by my excitement about the adventures ahead.

The next day we flew to Bombay. From the moment we arrived, we encountered chaos. People pushing their way in different directions, snaking through hundreds of stalls where vendors sold their wares. Trucks racing in an attempt to overtake the line of street cars. Overloaded double-decker buses with people hanging onto the sides, nearly overturning the vehicles. Coolies, their faces distorted with strain, trotting along with baskets and packages piled on their heads. Herds of buffalo, cows, and goats being driven along with sticks as their owners attempted to weave their way through the labyrinth of vehicles.

Cars, trucks, and buses all honked incessantly, as if trying to compete with one another. The noises were deafening.

The contrast between the tranquility and beauty of Beirut and the commotion of Bombay was striking, but I couldn't imagine being anywhere else. There was so much to learn and experience here.

When we got off the train in Lucknow, India, the sight of newly arrived American girls provoked a tidal wave of peddlers offering to sell us their wares. Inside the train station, the oppressive heat intensified the earthy smells of sweat, cooking oils, and urine.

I was thankful we didn't have to wait long before Miss Johnson, the prim and proper American teacher who would be our American liaison with the college, came riding up on her blue bicycle, white hair piled neatly on top of her head.

After introductions, she hired a rickshaw that took us through the downtown area, bustling with people, animals, and thick clouds of gas fumes. When we finally rode through the gate at Isabella Thoburn College, it was like entering a refuge. The sun's rays sparkled on whitewashed buildings, and gardens sprinkled throughout the campus emitted a strong fragrance of jasmine.

I asked Miss Johnson why there were so few students on campus. Wasn't school about to begin? After a moment of hesitation, she hit us with the news that school would be delayed for three weeks due to a flu epidemic all over India. During that time, we would not be allowed outside the walls of Isabella Thoburn College unless it was absolutely necessary.

We were disappointed that we wouldn't able to sightsee or travel. We spent most of those three weeks reading, writing letters to our loved ones back home, playing games, and swimming in the indoor pool.

The day after our quarantine ended, an American missionary family came by to meet us. Kit and Doug Stenger and their three daughters lived in a two-story, whitewashed stucco home in a quaint neighborhood near the college. "When campus life becomes overwhelming," Kit told us, "or if you just want to get away for some home-cooked American food, a listening ear, or straight talk, you're welcome to visit us."

Miss Johnson gave her a hug. "The Stengers have offered their home for several American girls in the past, and they've all found it very helpful."

We all thanked Kit and her husband enthusiastically.

I wrote love letters to Bill every day, and he wrote back faithfully. Every night, as I tried to sleep on the dorm's veranda, tucked beneath a mosquito net under the stars, I missed Bill terribly. His sense of humor. The way he could tell a story and make it come alive. How he laughed with his whole body. His compassion toward people. And most important, his loving acceptance of me.

And yet, as my friends and I explored India and its people, I sometimes worried that I didn't miss him enough.

When school finally started, there was little time to focus on anything except meeting the demands of our busy schedules. Everyone had to be up by 5:30. Breakfast was served promptly at 6:00. Chapel at 6:30. Class ran from 7:00 till 11:30. Lunch from noon to 2:00. From 2:30 to 3:30 was rest time, which was needed because of the oppressive mid-afternoon heat. We had tea at 3:30. From 4:00 to 5:30 we played field hockey or swam. Then we had free time until supper at 7:00. From 7:30 to 9:30 was study time. Lights out at 10:00.

There was never time to be bored. Or even lonely.

The citizens of India followed many religions, and it seemed they were always celebrating some type of holiday. On every one of them, the college sent the Indian girls home. We American girls joked that we managed to squeeze in a few classes between holidays. But that was fine by us, because that meant we could use those days to experience India firsthand, usually by train—in third class.

Having lived in Africa, I found India another exciting adventure to be experienced. Though there were stark differences between the two countries, India reminded me of Africa in many ways. Their citizens spoke several different languages and practiced multiple religions. Servants were the norm. In certain areas of both countries, kerosene lamps were the only source of light after sunset. India's mosquito nets, spicy foods, and hot climate also reminded me of my time in Africa. I soon came to love the country.

As the school year progressed, I wanted to share my experiences with Bill. So, I decided to invite him to come for a visit at Christmas time.

Of course, he couldn't stay in the girls' dorm with me. But my brother-in-law's parents, Ethel and Roady Roadarmel, were Baptist missionaries in Bhimphore, a small village in West Bengal, a few miles from Lucknow. I had met them several Christmases before at a family gathering in the States. I wrote and asked them if Bill and I could stay with them over the two-week Christmas break. To my delight, they responded that they would be pleased to have us spend our vacation with them.

When I told Kit Stenger about our plans, she pursed her lips. "You know, the Indian culture discourages dating. Bill won't be able to spend any private time with you during his visit at the college."

This seemed ridiculous to me. But out of respect to the Indian people, I agreed to follow Indian customs. Although I was disappointed, I wasn't surprised. The college was quite strict about not having young men on campus. The girls were never allowed to have boys visit them. But sometimes a young male "cousin" stopped by.

I stifled a giggle as I wrote my next letter.

Dear Bill,

Some wonderful missionaries here, the Stengers, have offered to pick you up at the airport in Lucknow and allow you to stay with them the first night. They will bring you to the college to see me. But you must pretend that we have never met. If anyone at the college found out we were dating, I would be kicked out.

I know that sounds strange, but I'll explain as soon as I see you.

All my love,
Jo

I felt sure Bill would have misgivings about traveling to India after reading that letter. But in spite of the extensive preparations—getting a passport and a visa, making expensive airplane reservations, to say nothing of the long, exhausting trip—he did come.

Kit Stenger brought Bill to the college the day after he arrived. When he got out of the car, I wanted to throw my arms around him and give him a kiss. Instead, I demurely shook his hand.

Despite my prior warnings, this perfunctory greeting seemed to shock Bill. Nevertheless, he smiled at me, and my heart pumped wildly.

We chatted for a while, and then I took him around the campus, Kit hovering a step or two behind us. I introduced Bill to the four other American girls and to some of my Indian friends as my "cousin." I ached to hold his hand. Knowing that was impossible made the situation feel awkward and contrived.

Kit invited me to come over for dinner so Bill and I would have a chance to talk privately. She served spaghetti with marinara sauce and garlic bread. Maybe not a special treat for Bill, but I devoured the good old American food.

After dinner, each of us carrying a lantern, Bill and I slipped out to the back veranda, where we made ourselves comfortable on the porch swing. We sat in silence for a while, listening to the distant sounds of the street.

Bill took my hand. "What are you thinking?"

"How thankful I am that you're here, and how excited I am to show you my India."

He pulled me close, and I hugged him until my arms hurt.

Laughter from the living room broke the silence. Knowing our time together was short, I reluctantly ended the embrace. "Before we go to Bhimphore, I'd like to take you to see Benares, the Holy City of the Hindus, and do some Christmas shopping in Calcutta."

"That sounds perfect."

With a sigh I stared at our interlaced fingers. "Unfortunately, unmarried couples can't travel together."

"What should we do about that?"

"I think, if anyone asks, we'd have to say that we're married."

Bill stood. "I'm not comfortable telling a lie, Jo."

I joined him. "I don't like it, either. But it's the only way for us to do anything together without offending the people here."

"Hopefully no one will ask," he mumbled.

Early the next afternoon, Kit picked me up in her car outside the gates of the college. Bill was waiting for me in the backseat. Since there was plenty of time before our train would be leaving for Benares, I asked Kit to drop us off at the entrance to the downtown bazaar.

Vendors offered every conceivable type of merchandise: sandals, shawls, newspapers, and all kinds of food and drink. I had been there many times, but I wondered if Bill would be overwhelmed by the mélange of sights and the cacophony of sounds. If he was, he kept it to himself.

After we wandered through the crowd for a while, one of the stalls caught Bill's eye. He stopped and pointed to the back wall, where an aqua sari with gold threads was hanging. "That's what I want to buy you for Christmas."

I loved his choice! I asked the vendor in Hindi how much it cost. When he replied, I said, "No, no, that is too much."

Bill looked horrified. He pulled me aside and whispered, "We can afford to pay that price."

"I know. But this is the way shopping is done in India."

With a few more rounds of bargaining, I got my Christmas gift.

After an hour or so amidst this fun and confusion, we got lost. When we finally found our way out of the bazaar, we hailed a rickshaw and told the driver we needed to get to the station quickly to catch our train. The bicycle-drawn cart wove precariously through the cyclone of trucks, buses, taxis, scooters, motorbikes, and other rickshaws in a whirl of collective madness. I prayed silently for our safety. Bill's white knuckles gripped the side of the rickshaw.

When we arrived at the station, we discovered we had missed our train. The next one going to Benares would not leave for another hour. As we exchanged our tickets for the later train, Bill discovered I'd made reservations in third class. "We'd like first-class passage, please." He forked over the extra money without batting an eye.

I had always traveled third class with my friends because we American girls wanted to experience the "real" India. The smell of bodies too long in the heat and coal dust. The Indian women standing stoically, eyes closed, not even enjoying the landscape as it sped past. There was no need to hang on to anything, because the press of bodies held us packed in like toy soldiers.

I was thankful for Bill's extravagance, especially since this would be an overnight trip. I wondered how different first class would be.

The crowded station's heat, combined with the strong smell of Indian food, forced us outside. There was no place to sit except on our luggage, which we plunked onto the platform. We were soon surrounded by curious children and other onlookers. I rather enjoyed the attention. We were an oddity, a young American couple traveling together. I wore my Indian Punjab outfit, a dress with ballooned pants. But Bill, in his blue jeans and T-shirt, stood out.

Our train arrived a half hour late. I assured Bill that was not unusual. He shrugged as we stepped onto the train and headed for our first-class compartment. It was dimly lit; a single light bulb hung from the wooden ceiling. The walls and floor emitted the smell of damp wood. On both sides of the room were narrow wooden bunk beds with blankets but no sheets or pillows.

Bill had just finished putting our luggage under one of the beds when a well-dressed Indian gentleman walked in. He strode over to us with a smile and introduced himself as Mr. Joshi. In perfect English, he told us that he was on his way home to see his wife and two children.

I wondered what he thought about a young American couple traveling together. And I worried that we might have to lie about being married.

A deafening whistle announced that the train was about to leave. The train lunged forward, almost throwing us to the floor. Mr. Joshi excused himself and returned to his side of the compartment. The train moved slowly down the tracks. After putting his luggage under the bed, Mr. Joshi opened his briefcase and began shuffling through his papers.

Bill climbed to the top bunk and I got onto the one below his. Even though I was dead tired, I was too keyed up to sleep, thinking about our day together and excited about being with Bill for the next couple of weeks.

After a few minutes, Bill's head popped down from the top bunk, and he looked at me upside down. "I can't wait till we get married," he said in a whisper that was loud enough for Mr. Joshi to hear.

With a frown, I put a finger to my lips. Realizing what he had said, he popped back to the top bunk. Neither of us spoke a word the rest of the night. I feared that we had revealed our secret. But the next morning our traveling companion was just as cordial as he had been the night before.

We arrived in Benares around 6:30 in the morning. After shoving our way through the crowded train station, we hailed a rickshaw. Our first stop was the Ganges, considered one of India's holiest rivers. I'd read that thousands of pilgrims came here to take a "holy dip" to wash away their sins.

We stood on the banks of the Ganges River, taking in the plethora of sights and sounds, while sweat poured from our foreheads. There were hundreds of people in the river: bathing, washing clothes, cleaning dishes, even drinking the water. On the shore, bodies were being cremated, the remains thrown into the river. A look of shock streaked across Bill's face.

"The Hindus believe the ashes eventually reach the ocean, where the currents take them away to eternity."

Bill shook his head. "Incredible."

Though the sight of people drinking contaminated water made my stomach churn, I felt closer to Bill than ever, grateful that we were able to share this experience.

After standing there for what seemed like hours, we visited one of the Hindu temples, then headed back to the train station. We would be leaving for Calcutta at 3:36 p.m.

I had read much about Calcutta, a city known for its beggars, people dying on the streets, famine, overpopulation, and poverty. It was the city where Mother Teresa and her Sisters of Mercy carried out their ministry to the poorest of the poor.

During my five months in India, I had learned to accept the things I could not change. There was little that shocked me anymore. I had come to terms with India for the intriguing country that she is. However, I was not prepared for what awaited us when we walked out of the train station in Calcutta. There, among the bicycle- and scooter-drawn rickshaws, a scrubby-looking, dark brown, half-naked man stood beside a small cart with wheels. Two men loaded their luggage and climbed aboard, then the dark man lifted it onto his back. The men were three times the size and weight of the man ready to carry them to the city. It seemed so inhumane.

Bill and I stood there, stunned. We couldn't bring ourselves to ride in a human-drawn rickshaw, even though this was a man's livelihood. Instead we found a rickshaw attached to a bicycle, paid the driver well, and headed for the city.

The rickshaw had a rhythm of its own as it weaved in and out around anything in its way. Dry, round little bushes, like tumbleweed, bounced over the road and collected on the other side. As we approached the downtown area, a purple sunrise peeked between patches of clouds. The night air had done little to cool the heat of the day. Our faces soon glistened with sweat.

The roadside stalls were just beginning to open for business when we arrived. Before our eyes, the city came alive with people, vehicles, animals, and lights, as if the curtain had just opened for a Broadway production. I was surprised to see Christmas lights strung on the stalls and shops, considering this was predominantly a Hindu and Muslin country. But the lights made me happy, reminding me of home.

The rickshaw driver dropped us off in the heart of the city. We were soon surrounded by curious children and street beggars. Bill reached into his pocket, but I grabbed his arm. He looked at me in surprise. "Jo, these children have so little. We can afford to give them a few rupees."

I shook my head. "If you give to one person, we'll be mobbed."

He frowned. I admired his desire to help the unfortunate. "We can give in other ways," I assured him. "The mission at Bhimphore accepts donations for the poor."

Bill shrugged. "I guess you're right."

When the beggars realized that we would not be giving them any money, they scattered to look for more gullible tourists.

We roamed from shop to shop, buying small gifts for friends and family. I enjoyed watching Bill learn the art of bargaining.

We caught another train at 4:15 p.m., arriving two hours later at the railway town of Kharagpur. Ethel Roadarmel picked us up in an open-air jeep owned by the mission station. Ethel was short and slightly plump, her dark hair streaked with white. She greeted us with a handshake and a warm smile. "We'll have to drive twenty-eight miles to the mission station," she said as she opened the back of the jeep. That was a long way to drive on unpaved roads.

Bill and I stowed the luggage and climbed into the two seats in the back. Gravel and dirt crunched under the wheels, and brown clouds of dust obscured the landscape. The open-sided jeep made conversation difficult, so we rode in silence. I gazed at the sights as we passed by. Women wearing colorful saris and carrying baskets of heavy loads on their heads. Children racing to the side of the road and waving at us. Cows, goats, and chickens wandering aimlessly through the villages.

Ethel swerved to avoid hitting some cow droppings that had not been removed from the road. "That dung will be collected by one of the local residents," she informed us. "Chopped straw will be added to it, and then it will be fashioned into cakes, dried in the sun, and used as fuel for cooking."

I had been aware of this, but Bill listened intently, his face stoic.

The sunlight began to disappear, casting an orange glow on the sides of the mud-and-straw huts. The smell of smoke drifted through the air, signaling that the local women were preparing the evening meal. I wondered if Bill was thinking about the use of cow dung in the preparation of their food.

It was close to 8:00 when we arrived at the mission station. The large, two-story, rectangular cement home had verandas and windows all around. Red and white bougainvillea lined the walkway to the front porch. It was far more spacious than I had expected, almost palatial. Certainly not what I'd expected for a home for missionaries. It looked more like the house of the chief in an African village.

Ethel must have seen the surprise on my face, because she hastened to tell us, "This house was originally intended for two families to live in."

A young boy of around thirteen greeted us at the front door, dressed in all-white, his bare feet slapping the floor of the cement porch as he scurried toward us. "*Namaste*," he said, joining his hands in the Indian gesture of greeting. He picked up our bags and headed for the second floor, placing them at the top of the stairs for us to retrieve later.

Ethel led Bill and me into the living area, where the warm, rich aroma of sandalwood mingled with the smell of kerosene. Persian rugs lay on polished teak floors. Soft light from several lanterns gave the area a sense of reverence. Indian artifacts filled the room: carvings in wood and marble, brass candy bowls and coasters, marble dishes inlaid with semiprecious stones.

Bill walked up to the fireplace. "Does it ever get cold here?"

I laughed, but Ethel didn't even crack a smile. "It can get quite cool during the winter season."

The smell of curry wafting from the kitchen reminded me that we hadn't eaten since early morning, when we had tea and biscuits at the railroad station. The cook had prepared a light meal of rice with curried sauce, and for dessert we were served an assortment of fruits, including mangos, bananas, and papayas. Conversation was also light as our bodies succumbed to the rigors of the day.

Ethel mentioned that her husband would be back from his pastor's conference the next morning. I had wondered where Roady was, eager for him to meet Bill. "There's a lot of work to do around here" she said. "Roady could sure use some help painting the woodwork at the church."

Bill had already realized that Ethel was a no-nonsense woman, so he wasn't surprised when she wanted to put him to work. He cheerfully offered to help in any way needed.

"And Jo," Ethel said, turning to me, "would you mind coming to the village with me to help with the children? I'll be teaching the women the beginning chapters of Luke, and we would all appreciate it if you could play some games with the children."

"I'd love that."

Bill winked. "Can Jo and I exchange jobs? I could play games with the kids and she could paint woodwork."

I cuffed his arm, and the three of us had a good laugh.

Following supper, Ethel showed us to our rooms. "Have a good night's rest." She smiled. "You'll need it."

After saying good night to Ethel and Bill, I closed my door and walked to the balcony. The moon, half hidden by clouds, dimly outlined the land surrounding the compound. A light wind caressed my face, reminding me of tender times with Bill. I prayed for us and for the world. Then, exhausted, I headed for bed and crawled under the mosquito net. The chirping of crickets through the open window lulled me to sleep.

The smell of paint and turpentine awakened me the next morning. I slipped on my bathrobe and peeked out the door. Bill was hurrying down the hall, fully dressed. He stopped when he saw me. "Roady's waiting for me in the car."

"I'll see you at the church."

The week was busy. When Bill wasn't painting woodwork in the church, he played volleyball with the village folks. During the village Christmas party, he passed around the microphone so each performer could be heard. On Sunday, Bill delivered the meditation for the church service.

I kept busy too, helping decorate the Christmas tree, cooking, and playing with the village children. The little ones, with their shiny faces and silky dark hair all came running to meet me whenever I showed up, pushing one another aside to get to me and touch my face. We played jacks with stones, and hide-and-seek. I loved every minute. But I wondered if Bill and I would ever have any time alone.

At the end of our first week in Bhimphore, the Roadarmels had a meeting at the church, and the servants finished their work early and went home, so Bill and I had the whole house to ourselves for the evening. We fixed some hot Darjeeling tea and set our cups on the copper coffee table in front of the wooden couch, where we sat among the many pillows covered with Indian fabric. The lanterns threw off soft light, enveloping the room in a muted glow. The living room felt peaceful, full of lovely crafts created by local artisans. The smell of kerosene brought back memories of my life in Africa, where we lived without electricity but with enough love to light up our lives.

Bill and I talked about our recent experiences, but the conversation soon turned to discussions about our future plans: where we would be married, where we'd like to live and go to church, and how I could help him in his ministry.

Suddenly, the wick of one of the lanterns burst into flame. Bill grabbed a copper bucket that was sitting on the side table and threw the water in it onto the lantern. It put out the flame, but it also broke the glass and shattered the delicate mantle.

I picked up the broken glass while Bill ran to his room to get a couple of handkerchiefs, which he used to sop up the water on the floor. How were we going to explain this to our hosts?

When Ethel and Roady returned from church, we told them what had happened. I hoped they would ease our guilt with a few words of comfort. Instead, a look of disgust crossed Ethel's face. "The lantern lost air pressure. It just needed to be pumped up."

Roady put an arm over her shoulder. "Ethel, it's our fault. We should have explained to them how this kind of lantern works." He turned to us. "Don't worry about it. Could have happened to anyone."

"We are very sorry," Bill said. "Can we buy you a new mantel?"

Ethel raised an eyebrow. "You'd have to travel all the way to Calcutta." Her lips pursed.

We held our breath, not sure how to respond. But after an uncomfortable moment, she winked at us. We all had a good laugh.

Bill's visit to India was not turning out to be the pleasant, relaxed interlude we had envisioned. We were both worn down by all the travel. And our frustration increased because we had so little time alone.

But there were still three precious days before Bill had to leave for the States. We reserved adjoining rooms in the beautiful Hotel de Paris in Bombay. I could hardly wait!

Our five-star hotel, its grand entrance adorned by a lavish crystal chandelier and a wide, curving staircase that seemed to lead straight to heaven, was our sanctuary for a few days, away from the noise, the smells, and the heat of the outside world. In the quiet of our hotel rooms, we had time to talk, to catch up, to reminisce about the places we had visited and the people we'd encountered. More important, we engaged in some much-needed straight talk, sorting through our feelings for each other.

Bill took my hand. "Over the last two weeks, you've kept me at a distance and expressed very little affection toward me. That makes me wonder if you're still in love with me."

Though I wanted to assure him, I confessed that I wasn't sure how I felt. Bill listened with patience as I voiced my thoughts and explored my emotions. We finally concluded that carrying on a courtship across two such different cultures was very difficult.

But as we spoke honestly with each other, our warm relationship came bubbling back. We resumed talking about the wedding, where we would live after we married, how many kids we wanted. The happy stuff. My feelings of love were rekindled, and we ended the night with soft kisses, warm embraces, and a re-commitment of our love for each other.

Bill would finish another semester at McCormick Seminary in Chicago. I would finish my studies at Isabella Thoburn College in five months and then head back to Berea College in Kentucky. While we were apart, we promised each other we'd stay connected through letters.

The next morning, Bill had to catch an early plane for the States. After a quick breakfast, he hailed a taxi. While we waited for it to arrive, we sneaked off to a little alcove around the side of the hotel. Hidden from sight, I took Bill's hands and he drew me close. As we held each other, I reveled in sweet memories of the past two days and nights. The experiences of the past two weeks still left me with some doubts about our fragile relationship. But I wasn't about to give up on our relationship.

When the semester finally neared an end, I decided to visit my mother, who was engaged in missionary work in Cameroon, West Africa, before heading to the United States. Since the other American girls were going straight to the States, I would be traveling alone. But that didn't bother me.

The hardest part was leaving my Indian friends from the college. They all came to say farewell before we American girls left. They gave us garlands, small gifts, and farewell kisses. It was especially heartbreaking saying good-bye to the choir, the student body, and the Stengers.

I shipped most of my belongings to Berea College, packed my remaining possessions in my well-worn bag, and flew from Calcutta to Rome, where I boarded a small Air France plane to Yaounde, the capital of Cameroon.

The aircraft's seats faced each other across a wide center aisle. I was the only female on the flight. The noisy, constant whirling of the propellers relaxed me, and I closed my eyes. Happy memories of Africa played in my head. I wondered if my childhood home would be very different now.

I was half awake when I looked up and saw a man standing in front of me. He was well groomed, rather handsome, middle-aged. "*Bonjour. Je m'appelle Pierre. Parlez-vous français?*"

"Very little," I replied in French.

Switching immediately to English, he asked what I planned on doing in Africa and why was I traveling alone.

"I'm visiting my mother. She's a teacher and missionary in Batouri. I also plan to visit my brother and his family, who live in Lolodorf."

A look of puzzlement came over Pierre's face. "I apologize. I thought you were one of the dancers who will be arriving today from the United States."

I don't know whether I felt complimented or insulted. Before he could explain why he'd approached me, the pilot announced that the plane would be landing soon. Pierre took his seat.

I looked out the window. The trees below looked like a field of Brussels sprouts. I held my breath as the plane came closer to the forest, afraid we might clip the treetops. We landed safely, and I grabbed my bag and headed for customs. Everyone else moved through without delay, but I was stopped at the entrance gate by a French official who asked me to wait. He and a guard spoke in rapid French, so I had no idea what the trouble was. Something about a missing form.

Before I could panic, Pierre came over to me. "Perhaps I can help." He spoke with the men in French. Then he turned to me. "You can go through now."

"What about the missing form?" I asked.

"It won't be needed after all."

I wondered briefly whether Pierre had engineered this as a way of getting better acquainted with me. Had he done this kind of thing before with other women? Feeling no need to find out, I thanked him, exited the airport as fast as possible, and headed toward the hotel.

Pierre caught up with me and asked if I would have dinner with him. I wasn't sure what his intentions might be. But I was grateful for his help at the airport. And I couldn't pass up a free meal. I agreed to meet him in the lobby at 6:00.

After checking into the hotel, I took the elevator up to my room and rested for about a half hour. Then I brushed my teeth, washed my face, and reapplied my makeup. Having nothing fancy to wear, I donned my white blouse and African print skirt.

Pierre was waiting in the lobby, and we walked down the hall to the hotel restaurant. I was surprised at how westernized and elegant it was. A maître d' escorted us to a table for two, with a white linen tablecloth and a candle glowing in a glass hurricane lamp. Pierre ordered a seven-course meal of lobster soup, salad with avocado, broiled shrimp, rare roast beef, lobster tails, fried chicken, and chocolate cake. While we ate, I chatted about my family and my experiences in India. Pierre was very attentive, but I had an uneasy suspicion that he might be expecting more from me than I was willing to give.

After dinner, feeling like a well-fed cat that wants to curl up for a nap, I thanked Pierre for the lovely meal, adding that I needed to retire because I had a long trip the next day. I headed for the elevator, hoping he wouldn't follow me. But he did.

We ended up on the elevator alone. He tried to kiss me, but I stepped back and told him I was not that kind of girl. He backed off. But I still felt a little uneasy. When the elevator reached my floor, I jumped out, hurried down the hall, rushed into my room, and locked the door behind me.

After a delicious breakfast at the Yaounde Hotel's café, I checked out and waited at the curb for my brother David. I hadn't seen him for two years, since he and his family were working in Africa. He was fifteen years older, so I was in grade school when he went off to college, followed by seminary. He slipped in and out of my life as I was growing up. We had lived in different places, worlds apart. He and his family lived just a half hour away from our mother's house. I couldn't wait to see them all.

David pulled up in a Ford station wagon. It was the same kind of car Bill drove, but my brother's was encrusted with dried mud. After welcoming me with a hug, he placed my bag in the back of the car while I slipped into the front seat.

Our father died when I was five, but I'd seen photographs of him. Like David, he had a high forehead and dark hair combed straight back without a part. David had followed in Dad's footsteps, even becoming a pastor and missionary in Africa.

For a while our conversation was strained. But when I asked about his children, he brightened up and talked about each one with deep affection.

The road to Batouri was unpaved, making travel slow. Billowing dust and stray animals wandered across the road, further impeding us. But those things actually made me smile. This was the Africa I remembered: traveling on dirt roads that turned to mud during the rainy season, miring cars in deep ruts, often leaving them stranded for hours. I felt thankful that on this day the weather was clear.

After a two-and-a-half-hour drive, David announced, "Mother's house is just around the bend."

A sea of yellow grasses lay like a carpet in front of the little concrete cottage. The edge of the field overlooked a valley where gold ore was mined. The landscape was beautiful. But with no one living nearby, I wondered if my mother was lonely.

No, I decided. She loved Africa, and her work. She would never have chosen a different life. Besides, Mother had always been a woman of strength and determination. At forty-nine, after Father died, she left her home and took my sister and me to Africa. I was seven, Ruth nine. That took lots of courage.

When David and I arrived at the house, Mother ran out to greet us. I flew out of the car and threw my arms around her. Uncomfortable with the show of affection, she herded us inside to get settled.

Walking into the cottage was like taking a step back into my childhood. Wicker furniture with seat pillows covered in floral fabric. A small corner cupboard displaying the beautiful hand-painted china my father had given her. Oriental rugs throughout. I stood there for a moment, taking it all in. Mother showed me to the guest bedroom, and I dropped off my bag and headed for the small dining room, where she had tea and sugar cookies waiting. We talked about my trip and about India until the sky turned dark and it was time for David to go home.

I stayed in Africa for a month, visiting the boarding school I'd attended for several years and spending time with David and his family. My nieces, Mary Beth and Debby, giggled when I told them about my encounter with Pierre and asked me to repeat the story over and over. My stay was filled with banter and laughter.

I spent most of my time with Mother on the hill overlooking the countryside, talking about my year in India and her life in Africa. I wrote letters to Bill, and Mother sewed.

A few days into my visit, I received a letter from Pierre. I was shocked. How had he gotten my mother's address? I certainly didn't give it to him. The letter was written in French, so I asked Mother to translate it. Instead, she tore it up and threw it away. I was disappointed, curious about what he had to say. But my mother would not have reacted the way she did if Pierre hadn't written something wildly inappropriate.

Still . . . I have often wondered what was in that letter.

I was sweaty and tired when my plane landed at O'Hare in Chicago. But Bill was waiting for me with a bouquet of red roses, and suddenly I felt like a princess in a ball gown. As I ran to meet him, his expression of eager anticipation changed to one of surprise and disappointment.

I knew why. I'd had a New York beautician cut my long hair short. Bill had always loved my hair long, but after having all my split ends snipped off and getting a soft perm, there wasn't much length left. In addition, all the potatoes, curries, and Indian sweets I'd eaten had added thirty pounds to my body. I looked more like an old-maid school teacher than the beautiful young student he'd said good-bye to eight months before.

Bill gave me a hug without saying a word about my hair or my girth. I thanked God for a man who loved me enough not to comment about the change in my physical appearance.

Before Bill and I got married. I wanted to return to Berea College to see my old friends—one in particular.

Ray and I had dated almost from the day I arrived at Berea. I'd been drawn to this attractive guy who dominated the basketball court, his thick brown hair disheveled as he ran. He seemed to glide rather than walk through the doors of the dorm whenever he came to pick me up for a date. I loved being tucked against his tall, lean body as we danced during our lunch hour almost every school day at the Hang Out.

Ray had one talent for which I took credit. I had been involved in the drama department at Berea. We were planning to put on a play, *The Barretts of Wimpole Street,* and we needed a Robert Browning. I told Ray he'd be perfect for the role since he was so tall and handsome.

When I encouraged him to try out, he said, "No way. The guys on the team would make fun of me."

"So what? This could be fun for you." I kept after him until he finally relented.

As I suspected, he landed the part. And he loved doing it. Whether it was the adulation of the crowd or the love of playing different characters that intrigued him, Ray was hooked on acting from that first performance. In college he played the lead role in many dramas, and he later became a professional actor, performing in movies and plays in New York City.

I wasn't sure how I felt about Ray now, but I couldn't marry Bill until I knew. I needed to find out by going back to Berea.

When I mentioned this to Bill, he put on a brave face. But I could tell from the sullen tone in his voice that he had been patient enough with me and was seriously considering breaking up over this.

In spite of the risk, I went back to Berea. I was at the swimming pool when Ray found me. We had a date that evening, and I knew immediately that my feelings for him were nothing compared to what I felt for Bill. Ray asked me to marry him that night. I told him, gently, that I was in love with someone else. I could hardly wait to get back on the bus and return home.

Bill was waiting for me at the station. When I stepped off the bus, he didn't kiss me. Instead we stood in awkward silence, then walked to the car without saying a word. We hadn't driven far when Bill asked, "What have you decided?"

I took his hand. "I love you, Bill, and I want to marry you."

He almost ran off the road. Instead, he pulled over to the side and threw his arms around me. "I can't tell you how I sweated this out."

"I know. And I'm sorry." I admired him more than ever for his restraint, his courage, and his patience.

3

I was deeply grateful for Bill's patience throughout my studying in India and my returning to Berea. My past was now in order, nothing left undone. The future lay ahead like the blank pages of a diary.

During the weeks leading up to August 2, 1958, I made last-minute preparations for one of the most important days in my life: my wedding.

Neither of my parents would be present for the ceremony. Father had died, and Mother was still involved in Africa. I felt sad that she wouldn't be at my wedding, but the timing was right for my life.

I invited two substitute moms to be at the ceremony: my sister Miriam and Bill's mother. Miriam brought a spirit of joy to any occasion. She had a way of making everyone feel good about themselves.

Bill's mom helped me with the myriad of things a mother and daughter do before a wedding. I loved my own mother, who was independent, self-assured, determined. Her work in Africa had eternal value, but it consumed her life. Bill's mom, on the other hand, centered her life on her family. I enjoyed shopping with her, going out to lunch, and learning her cooking secrets. I was especially thankful for her help with wedding preparations. She never questioned any of my decisions.

My brother Jack agreed to step in for my father. Jack was tall and slender, quite handsome, with thick, dark hair. I was proud to have him walk me down the aisle.

My Indian friends lived too far away to attend, and my Berea buddies didn't have the money to travel that far, nor the time to take away from their jobs. But I was happy that four bridesmaids and a few family members agree to come.

Gini, my maid of honor, would be arriving the day before the wedding from New York State. I had met her at Chautauqua, where we roomed together at the Presbyterian House. Laura and Inky, friends from Berea, were traveling by bus from different towns in Kentucky. Fran, my fourth bridesmaid, was the wife of a friend of Bill's from seminary, and soon would become my friend.

Bill and I had chosen an August wedding date, and I wanted the ceremony to reflect the soft colors of summer. My bridesmaids would wear long, princess-style taffeta dresses in pastel colors of baby blue, pink, yellow, and moss green. I couldn't afford to pay for the girls' dresses, so I sent them a pattern, with instructions of what material they should buy.

My wedding dress was borrowed from Bill's cousin. It was white with a long satin skirt covered in lace, fitted at the waist, with a high neckline and long sleeves. It was a perfect fit, as if it had been made just for me. I felt beautiful in it.

On the day before the wedding, I picked up Inky from the bus station. She alighted from the Greyhound with a sheepish look on her face. As I gave her a warm hug, she whispered, "I'm so sorry, Jo, but someone stole my bridesmaid's dress. I put it on the rack above my seat when I boarded. But when I looked for it, it was gone."

Who on earth would steal a bridesmaid's dress? Especially when the owner was sitting right beneath it!

I hugged my friend tighter and assured her that something would happen to solve the problem. But I wasn't sure what.

When word got out about the theft, Mrs. Hall—one of the saints of the church, a big supporter of Bill's and the woman who'd hosted a wedding shower for us—called him and offered to sew an identical dress for Inky. When he told me the news, I shed tears of relief and gratitude, but I said, "Bill, the wedding is the day after tomorrow. Can she get it done in one day?"

"She believes she can. But you'll have to get her the pattern and the material right away."

Bill's mother and I immediately headed downtown, looking for the same material as the original. We looked in every fabric and department store in town. At the last shop in the city, we finally found the matching material. We rushed back to Mrs. Hall's home so she could begin her mission of mercy. She spent all night sewing Inky's dress.

One of the families of the church invited my bridesmaids and me to stay in their home the night before the wedding. I had never met them; they were spending the summer at their cottage in the Upper Peninsula of Michigan. It was a large home, so each bridesmaid would have her own room. By the time all the bridesmaids had arrived at the house, it was late, and after brief introductions we retired to our rooms.

But I couldn't sleep. Scattered thoughts kept intruding. *Bill is a good man, and there are many reasons to marry him. He's kind and gentle. He is going to be a pastor. I love his parents. I will be financially secure. But am I madly in love with him?*

I had dated many guys who had helped me figure out what I wanted in a husband. According to my list of requirements and wishes, Bill was perfect. But I had to confess to myself that the passionate emotional bond I'd always assumed would be part of my relationship with my husband wasn't there with Bill.

Then I remembered India, where marriages are often arranged, and the couples fall in love as time passes. I knew marrying Bill was right for me and that someday I would fall passionately in love with this man.

After wrestling with my thoughts, I finally fell asleep.

The next morning, I awoke refreshed, ready for the day. I looked at my watch and realized that I had overslept. As I jumped out of bed, I heard loud chatter down the hall. I slipped into my bathrobe and slippers and headed for Inky's room. She gave me a bright smile, which surprised me. Was she confident that her dress would arrive on time, or was she acting calm for my benefit? Before I could ask how she was doing, the doorbell rang.

"I'll get it," I yelled, then ran down the stairs and opened the front door. Mrs. Hall stood on the porch, holding the finished taffeta dress, beautifully pressed. I threw my arms around her, almost knocking us both over.

"Thank you, thank you, thank you, Mrs. Hall! How can I ever repay you?"

Her eyes misted over. "Just love our Bill as we do."

I ran back upstairs, the pink dress draped carefully over both arms. Inky's face lit up. She lifted it high above her head, waltzed down the hallway, and disappeared into her room while the rest of us clapped our approval.

Back in my bedroom, my beautiful white wedding dress hung on the back of the door. As I stood there admiring it, there was a knock at the door. In walked my maid of honor.

"Oh, Gini, I'm so glad you're here! Can you help me put on my dress?"

"Of course." She carefully slipped it over my head. When she had finished buttoning all the buttons in the back, I stood in front of the mirror, and I must admit I liked what I saw. When I finally pulled my eyes from the reflection, I saw my bridesmaids gathered in the hall. They looked stunning in their dresses. And Inky's matched the others' perfectly.

They gathered around me, exuding approval. While I was basking in all the attention, the doorbell rang, and my brother Jack stuck his head through the front door. "Anyone ready to go to the church?"

Squeals of delight echoed throughout the house while the girls picked up their skirts and hustled down the stairs. I remained at the top and waved to Jack.

He smiled, then turned to the girls. "I'll drop you off at the church so you can help the youth group with the reception. Then I'll come back to pick up Jo."

Jack returned for me half an hour later. A soft breeze helped mitigate Indiana's sweltering heat. I had to hold on to my headpiece to keep it from slipping off or messing up my hair.

Streaks of purple crossed the blue sky as Jack drove me to the church. I prayed for my future with Bill. Excitement built as we came closer to the church.

The Forty-Third Avenue Presbyterian Church, with its limestone exterior, looked formal but not pretentious. Bill had worked as a student pastor there for the past two years, and this was where our lives would be united. Jack let me out at the bottom of the stairs leading up to the main entrance. While he parked the car, I picked up the hem of the lacy white skirt and ran up the stairs. I waited for him at the top, welcomed by carvings on either side of the heavy wooden door. On one side, carved in limestone, Jesus stood with outstretched arms; on the other side was a family gathered together. The carvings announced to visitors that everyone who walked through those doors would be welcomed.

Jack scrambled up the limestone stairs and grabbed the brass handle, opening the door to the next chapter of my life. My bridesmaids were in the lobby, waiting for me. They adjusted my headpiece, which had almost been dislodged by the summer breezes.

Jack left for the kitchen to get a cup of coffee, while I peeked inside the sanctuary, where the wedding would take place. Rays of sunlight streamed through the stained-glass windows at the front of the church, streaking across the communion table. Candles and baskets of daisies adorned the front of the sanctuary. The rich sound of organ music filled the air. As guests started to arrive, I headed for the dressing room to wait with my bridesmaids.

After everyone else was seated, Jack returned and led us to the back of the sanctuary. One of Bill's groomsmen escorted his parents to their seats at the front of the church. Then they led my sister Miriam to the seat reserved for the mother. After she was seated, the organist played Bach's "Jesu, Joy of Man's Desiring," the cue for the bridal procession to begin. The bridesmaids, holding bouquets of yellow and white daisies, walked in a row down the polished limestone aisle, their taffeta skirts dancing playfully behind them.

Gini, my maid of honor, went last. Her blue taffeta dress perfectly complemented her blonde hair and blue eyes. When she reached the front of the sanctuary, the organist pulled out all the stops—literally—for Mendelssohn's "Wedding March."

I slipped my hand through Jack's arm and we began the long walk to the front, the white skirt of my wedding gown swishing gracefully around me. As we passed row after row of smiling faces, I was stunned to see so many people at the ceremony. But this was Bill's church, his "family," and they cared about him. The only people I knew were the women who had attended my wedding shower and the young people Bill worked with. But everyone smiled at me, and I smiled back. Halfway down the aisle, I spotted Mrs. Hall and her husband. When our eyes met, I blew her a kiss and mouthed, "Thank you!"

Bill's loving eyes followed me all the way down the long aisle of the sanctuary. He looked sharp in his tailored white jacket and dark blue pants. When I got close, our eyes connected. A sense of calm surrounded me, and I knew I was doing the right thing. I looked forward to our life together.

Radiant faces welcomed me when I reached the front of the sanctuary. Two men stood beside my husband-to-be: Pastor Shults, Bill's minister in Terre Haute, where Bill had begun his journey into the Christian faith; and Dr. Goodpasture, Bill's boss and friend.

Bill took my hand, his face flushed and grinning. I stood close to him while the pastors conducted the service. As we knelt for prayer, there was no question in my mind that marrying Bill was right. When Pastor Shults announced, "You may now kiss your bride," Bill lifted my veil and with gentle intention kissed my lips.

Majestic music burst forth. My new husband and I whirled around to see a church filled with happy faces. I latched onto Bill's arm with one hand, picked up my wedding skirt with the other, and we floated down the aisle, beaming. Downstairs, at a reception in the fellowship hall, we welcomed family and friends, both old and new.

4

After the wedding reception, Bill and I climbed into his blue-gray Plymouth and headed off for our honeymoon. Bill's parents had offered us their cottage in Kentucky, where we could rest and dream about the future. We had planned to drive all the way that evening, but after about an hour, fatigue and excitement took its toll. So we stopped at a motel.

When I walked into our room, my heart sank. It was hardly big enough for a double bed, without a headboard. A bare light bulb hung from the low ceiling, paint was peeling from the walls, and the carpet smelled like well-worn gym shoes. Not what I would have chosen for our first intimate night together.

Our parents had never talked to us about sex. When I asked my mother whether her six children had been planned, she blushed. Subconsciously, she implanted the idea in my head that sex was something to be ashamed of. This made my first experience as a wife awkward and uncomfortable.

The next morning, on the two-hour ride to Kentucky, Bill talked nonstop, but I couldn't think about anything but the night before. *Bill should have planned better. That's the groom's responsibility.*

I stared out the window, watching the cars speed by, wishing I could wash away the memory of my first night as a married woman.

Bill's voice interrupted my thoughts. "I'm so excited about spending time at Mom and Dad's cottage." He talked about all the things we would do there. He spoke with such passion that I started to get excited about what lay ahead, anticipating days of rest and relaxation among beautiful surroundings.

It was close to noon when we arrived at the little red-and-white cottage with the screened-in porch. The smell of freshly picked flowers greeted us when we opened the side door leading to the living area. Roses from Bill's mother's garden sat on the wicker table, with candles on each side. Bill's mother had stuffed the freezer with casseroles, cookies, and coffee cakes.

For two weeks, Bill and I relaxed and enjoyed each other. We read books and wrote hundreds of thank-you notes for wedding gifts. We sat on the porch and gazed down the hill at the little fishing lake tucked among the canopy of willow trees. Some afternoons, Bill grabbed his fishing gear from the dusty garage and headed to the lake. He never caught enough for dinner, but that didn't matter. He had fun.

The relaxed atmosphere, and Bill's gentleness and patience, gradually diminished my feelings of dread and discomfort when it came to the sexual aspect of our relationship.

After two weeks of intimate togetherness, we headed for Indiana. I was not looking forward to our arrival in Logansport. I thought of Indiana as provincial, boring, behind the times. After all, I had lived in Africa, studied in India, and traveled around the world. But Bill was excited about taking over a parish there that needed a pastor for three churches, so of course I didn't express my feelings.

Soon after our arrival, I learned that Indiana was a state with great plains, basketball mania, corn fields that stretched as far as the eye can see, and farm houses sprinkled between weathered barns, exposing large expanses of sky. But the town of Logansport was dreary and dull, as though time had stopped there around the 1930s. Our home and the three churches we would be serving were in the country.

As we drove out of town on Route 25, I saw in the distance a beautiful building with a white exterior and well-maintained grounds. A quaint sign identified it as the Bethlehem Presbyterian Church. Right next to it was the manse, the little white ranch-style house where we would live. A circular driveway wound around the front of the house, and flowers peeked out everywhere. I had lived in so many different places that a home of our own fulfilled a deep longing in my heart. Even though it belonged to the church, it would be ours at least for a few years.

I could hardly contain my excitement when we walked in the front door. Everything sparkled. Bill told me the church members had put in a new furnace, painted the walls, and refinished the hardwood floors. I stood in the middle of the living room, taking it all in. Bill walked over and put his arms around me. Without a word being said, I knew we had made the right decision to live and serve in Indiana.

The next day, Bill and I headed for downtown Logansport to look for living room furniture. We felt like two kids who'd been let loose in a candy store! We had been careful with the money Bill had saved by buying some things secondhand, like a used mattress for the extra bedroom. But when it came to the living room, we bought exactly what we wanted. Early American seemed the perfect furniture for the living room's hardwood floors and large front window. We found a beautiful round braided wool rug in muted oranges and browns that felt warm and inviting.

A whole new life was about to begin for us. Were we prepared to handle all the adjustments of a new marriage and pastoring three churches?

No one in my family lived anywhere near Indiana. Mother and my brother and his family were still in Africa. My other siblings were scattered all over the United States. But Bill and I were welcomed into a new, larger family—the church family.

The folks at all three churches felt it was their responsibility to make sure the young pastor and his wife got off to a good start in their ministry. Many of the members treated us like part of their own families. Along with their gentle guidance came lots of love, expressed in many ways: gifts from their gardens, meat from animals they had raised and slaughtered themselves, praise for Bill's sermons, and encouragement of my singing and speaking.

The congregation also had some unusual ways of making us feel welcome. Shortly after we moved into the parsonage, we were about to sit down to dinner in the small dining room. An orange-and-yellow table cloth covered the antique table we had purchased for $50. Hamburgers and burnt potatoes were on the menu that night. (I never learned to cook. In Africa our cook wouldn't let me near his kitchen, and I spent my growing-up years in boarding schools and college dorms, with no access to a kitchen.) Bill and I had just finished putting the food on the table when a terrifying sound came from the front yard: shouting, pots and pans banging, and the continuous blast of car horns.

"What's happening?" I shouted, knocking over my chair as I stood. Were we about to be attacked by a mob in pickup trucks and tractors?

Bill ran around the house looking out windows. As I was about to panic, Martha Baker, a church member, stuck her head in the back door and shouted, "You're being belled." She and several other church members piled into our small kitchen. The shocked expressions on our faces brought roars of laughter from the invading troops.

Another moment of panic came when someone called out, "Are you ready to feed this crowd?"

I couldn't possibly handle a meal for all these folks. Not without a miracle of multiplying loaves and fishes. Fortunately, Martha had brought plenty of candy bars, chips, and popcorn.

"Jo and Bill," she announced, "we are honoring you with our first old-fashioned shivaree in ten years."

Someone else explained, "*Shivaree* is a French word. It means a noisy serenade for newlyweds."

"If this was the eighteen hundreds," said Albert Rodgers, a church elder, "shotgun blasts would have shattered the silence tonight."

Bill glanced at me with a nervous look. Sensing our discomfort, Martha put her arms around me and smiled. "Tonight, you are going to experience our version of a shivaree." Then she announced in a loud voice, "Now the king and queen must take their throne."

We were led outside and put in the back of an open truck. Everyone piled into tractors, trucks, hay wagons, anything that moved and was open to the elements. We all wound our way around the countryside on narrow gravel roads that ran alongside corn fields ready for harvest. Everyone banged on pots, pans, kettles, and shovels, or blew horns and other things that made noise. Shouting and laughter filled the night air. Finally, we arrived at the home of one of the church members, and everyone piled inside.

The women of the church knew how to cook. The table was soon brimming with homegrown green beans with bacon, fresh sweet corn, tomatoes right out of the garden, beef and noodles, chicken and noodles. My little hamburgers and burnt potatoes couldn't compete with this beautiful display of food.

After a time of fun and laughter, we headed for our homes with full stomachs. And full hearts.

It took a while for Bill to make the adjustment from the academic world of the seminary to a world of live people with real problems. When the ruling body of the church stressed the importance of regularly visiting all of the church members, Bill politely stated that he wasn't called to the ministry for that purpose. He had more important things to do: studying, preaching, teaching, making sure the administrative responsibilities were taken care of.

I could see the value of making personal connections, so I offered to go with him on his visits. "I think it'll be fun."

He finally relented, and we made a few afternoon calls. I enjoyed getting to know the people we were serving, hearing about their lives. Even mundane things like crop rotation and milking the Black Angus cows. I particularly liked learning the woman's cooking secrets. And I was especially pleased when the conversations shifted to world affairs.

Bill tried to act interested in long explanations of how milking machines worked and whether the crops would thrive without enough rain. Whenever I saw his eyelids slowly closing, I poked him gently with my elbow, hoping no one noticed.

After a few months, he began to enjoy these visits. Mainly because he realized the connection between getting to know people and having them listen to what he had to say on Sunday mornings.

Bill spent most mornings working on his sermons in the study, which was at the front of the house, where he could look out the window and watch traffic speeding by. This was his sanctuary.

But preaching was what he loved most about his work. It came naturally for him, even though he worked hard on his content and delivery. I felt blessed to have married a man with such an exceptional gift for preaching, and the church also reaped the benefits. Attendance on Sunday mornings began to exceed the number of members as guests flocked in.

I looked forward to hearing Bill preach, proud of my husband as he stood confidently in the pulpit, speaking with authority. His sense of humor often came out when he was preaching. His deep hurt over human injustice thundered with outrage. And his sense of God's compassion in the midst of life's troubles flowed like a cool, bubbling stream. His sermons seemed to come from a place deep within, from a man older and wiser than his years, a man who had already experienced suffering.

But Bill's sermons weren't always appreciated. In 1961 he felt called to give a sermon on the theme "A Roman Catholic in the White House." Richard Nixon was running for president against John F. Kennedy, an avowed Catholic, and many U.S. citizens were saying that, if Kennedy were president, the United States would be controlled by the Pope. Bill said in his sermon that the only issue for Christians was to elect whichever candidate stood most clearly for justice and love. He wasn't very popular that Sunday, or for several weeks after.

Bill often spoke about his preaching professor, Dr. Anthony King, a black pastor who had several pastorates in New York. Bill felt that Dr. King was exactly what the Preaching Department at McCormick Seminary needed: someone who was aware of humankind's predicament. Dr. King would tell his students, "Our first concern in preaching is what we are. What we say doesn't mean a thing unless we are what we say. Therefore, your first assignment every day is to have devotions." This became a road map for Bill's life.

My husband lived what he preached, and prayer became an integral part of his life.

Bill and I continued to adjust to married life, trying to understand each other's routines and habits. He was meticulous—everything had to be in its place, including his huge collection of books, lined up on the shelves with perfect precision. I was much more relaxed about clutter, partly as a result of having lived away from home during my growing-up years.

Bill never seemed to get angry, which seemed unnatural to me. During my year in India I had suppressed my feelings, reasoning that it was inappropriate to display anger in front of the Indian girls. After all, we were ambassadors of our faith and our country. But I firmly believed in expressing honest emotions with close friends and family members.

Bill told me about something from his childhood that explained why he was so afraid to show anger. "The summer I was thirteen, as we were getting ready for our Michigan vacation, Mother got mad at me because I was practicing with my fishing rod instead of packing. She gave me the silent treatment for two and a half hours. I kept begging her to say something. She gave me nothing but a stone face. I wished she would yell at me—that would have been less painful. After that, I never allowed myself to be angry. And I tried hard to make sure she never got angry with me."

I decided that when a suitable opportunity arose, I would teach my husband the art of how to express one's anger. My chance came one chilly March morning. We had just finished breakfast, and I handed Bill a dishtowel. He scrunched up his forehead. He'd been awake until 2:30 in the morning after the previous night's board meeting. Helping me with the dishes was the last thing he wanted to do, but he knew I needed to talk. So he took the towel.

"I wish you could have your meetings in the church instead of in our dining room," I began, scrubbing bits of egg off a frying pan. "I could hear everything that was being said, even though I was at the far end of the house."

Bill sighed. "Meeting here saves fuel. Besides, the house is church property."

I handed him the wet pan. "Maybe you're just too lazy to change things." I laughed.

"You know I'm not afraid to confront people when necessary."

"Then what's your problem?"

Bill crouched down to put away the pan in a low cupboard. "I don't have a problem."

"Oh, yes, you do. Last night you complained that I didn't have a hobby. The night before that, you lectured me about using too much toothpaste. What's really bugging you?"

He stood, his face red.

"You look angry. Are you upset with me?"

"No," he insisted.

I squeezed my soapy dish rag on top of his head, certain the foamy water dripping down his face would force him to let his fury out. Instead, his fingers clenched into fists. Was he about to hit me?

Fearing I had gone too far, I ran down the hall to our bedroom. Bill followed right behind me, but not fast enough to stop the door from slamming in his face. I flipped the lock. He beat on the sturdy plywood, sputtering, "Let me in."

I said nothing.

"Come on, Jo!" he shouted with obvious frustration and irritation.

I remained silent.

I heard Bill's footsteps run down the hall. About ten minutes after the sound faded away, I heard twisting and pounding noises outside the door, as if he were trying to loosen the hinges.

Bill had no aptitude for anything mechanical. And his anger undoubtedly made the challenge more difficult.

Finally, pieces of the wooden frame split loose from the hinge. When it gave way, my husband stood in the doorway, holding a crowbar, with a screwdriver, hammer, and pliers lying at his feet.

I lay on the bed, pretending to read a magazine. But out of the corner of my eye, I watched Bill march into the room and discover the handwritten Scripture quotations I'd placed on the floor leading up to the bed.

"Blessed are the peacemakers."

"Love your enemies."

"Be reconciled one to another."

The last note lay on the bed next to my feet. It read, "A good woman is hard to find."

Bill stood there, hands on his hips. I detected the beginning shadow of a grin, and we both burst into laughter. With his anger gone, he lay down on the bed, snuggled up close, and professed his love for me.

That evening at dinner, I confessed to Bill the reason for my little charade. "I was trying to get you to express your anger."

"Well, it worked," he replied.

5

Bill and I had been married less than a year when I discovered I was pregnant. I loved the prospect of having a child, though the prospect of months of nausea diminished my enthusiasm a little.

I assumed Bill would be elated too. And he did try hard to match my excitement. But I sensed he was pretending. Was he holding something inside?

One balmy afternoon in July, I had just awakened from a nap and was reaching for a Saltine cracker, hoping to minimize the queasy feeling in my belly, when Bill walked in with an expression on his face that I didn't recognize. He looked confused, almost fearful. When he started to put his arms around me, I said, "Not now, honey. I'm not feeling well."

He gripped my upper arms and drew me to himself forcibly. I pushed him away, but he held me with fierce determination. "This is my marital right."

Had I heard him correctly? Was he really going to force me to have sex with him?

When I continued to refuse him, he grew increasingly irritated, and I became more frightened. Where was the gentle Bill I had always known?

After several more attempts to persuade me he finally gave up and walked back to his study.

One night, I awoke to find him pacing the floor in the bedroom. "Why are you up so late?" I asked with a yawn, irritated at having been awakened from a pleasant dream.

"I can't sleep. I can't stop thinking. My mind won't slow down."

I saw terror in his eyes. But I had no point of reference for this. "What are you thinking about?" I asked, hoping we could make this quick so I could get back to sleep.

He stopped pacing and faced me, but averted his eyes from mine. "Will the baby take away your love from me?"

How could he even think that?

Praying silently, I got out of bed and walked over to him. I placed my cool hand on his flushed cheek. "Bill, no one could ever do that."

He resumed pacing. "In a year or so, I could be serving the largest church in the country."

What did that have to do with our baby or my love for him? He didn't elaborate, just started babbling about so many different topics all at once I couldn't keep track of them all.

"Jo, I'm starting to believe that I'm Jesus."

What on earth?

He continued on with more nonsense. As I stared at Bill, pacing and mumbling, fear gripped my heart. My husband was having a mental breakdown.

I didn't know what to do. I couldn't ask anyone for help— certainly no one in the church, not even my family. I didn't want them to think less of Bill. Knowing that Bill's parents had been through an earlier breakdown with him, I called them. They persuaded me to take him to a hospital close to them so he could receive treatment from Dr. Jacobson, the physician who had initially treated him. I asked the church for vacation time, which they granted, no questions asked. And, in spite of his delusional thoughts, Bill realized that he needed help and agreed to check in to the hospital for a rest.

We packed the car and headed for Cincinnati. While Bill was in the hospital, I stayed with his parents at their cottage in Ryland Lakes Country Club in Kentucky, where we'd spent our honeymoon. I was five months pregnant and still experiencing nausea, so I was very grateful for their care. But part of me blamed them for his illness. If they hadn't taught him to suppress his anger all the time, perhaps this wouldn't have happened.

Bill spent three weeks in the hospital. Through daily psychotherapy sessions, and with the help of medication, Bill began to see that his negative thoughts about the baby were normal resentments toward a rival for his love. He was relieved when the doctor said, "It's OK to think terrible things. Thoughts don't kill."

When we came back home, we weren't sure whether the church knew the reason for our "vacation." Had there been gossip? Would Bill have to gain the respect of everyone all over again? But when we returned, the people welcomed him back with open arms and hearts. He was accepted again as their leader, wounded but no less capable.

The routine of life resumed. Bill continued to work hard at his preaching while I prepared for the new baby. A week before my due date, December 4, 1959, Bill's mother came to help. I loved having her with us, doing what she enjoyed most: cooking. Every day, coffee cakes and casseroles lined the kitchen counters, and chicken-noodle soup bubbled away on the stove. But my due date came and went, with no sign of our firstborn. So, she stored her gifts in the freezer. At least I was learning to cook at the feet of a master.

Excitement built while we waited. A week went by, then two, and still no baby. Bill's mother returned to Cincinnati to attend to her husband, who knew little of how to survive without a wife, even though he was the vice president of a successful national company.

A week later Bill's mother came back, believing the baby would surely arrive soon. She brought loads of Christmas gifts. She always began her Christmas shopping early, hunting for bargains throughout the year. This resulted in a bountiful hoard of colorfully wrapped gifts purchased at bargain-basement prices.

Christmas presents had never been plentiful when I was growing up in the African rain forest. Our sponsoring churches from the States would send us a few gifts and an assortment of hard candies, which we opened sparingly throughout the year. So, on this Christmas in Logansport, Indiana, I felt like a child who had been dropped into a dream. Our home was full of reminders of the season: music, a decorated tree, the smell of cookies baking. And the expectation of a baby.

Bill's father arrived at our home on Christmas Eve, hoping for a hot meal. Instead, he found us at the hospital, where we had been most of the day.

At 9:00 on Christmas morning, after twenty-six hours of exhausting labor, we received a precious gift: a beautiful baby girl. No one could have been more excited than her father.

I had expected a blue-eyed, fair-skinned, bald-headed child. Instead, Rebecca had loads of dark hair, and her skin looked as if she had spent time in the sun. She was perfect. Even before she was cleaned up, the doctor handed her to Bill. He held her in his arms and wept. When the nurse took her to the nursery, my husband parked himself in front of the window, staring into the room where she slept.

Becky was the kind of baby any parent would wish for. She was calm and good, slept through the night, never spit up. She was totally cute and lovable. We thoroughly enjoyed being her parents, finding it difficult not to spoil her.

Even as a two-year-old, Becky warmed people's hearts. She was everyone's friend, smiling at the folks in the pews, sharing hugs and kisses for those with outstretched arms.

There was much I needed to learn about being a mother, and the women of the church were always ready to help and give advice. One day in midsummer, I was in the kitchen washing dishes, with Becky playing at my feet. A carton of bottled pop sat on the kitchen counter. Deciding to keep her busy putting the bottles in and out of the slots, I set the carton on the floor in front of her. The room resounded with my child's happy laughter while I turned my mind to all the things that had to be done that day.

A loud bang reverberated throughout the kitchen. My hands flew to my mouth as I gasped for air. One glass bottle had slammed against another, and the carbonation triggered an explosion, sending pieces of glass flying everywhere. One shard flew into Becky's forehead, spattering blood everywhere.

I yelled for Bill, who was working in his office at the front of the house, to bring something that would blot up the blood. I scooped Becky up in my arms and searched frantically for any other wounds.

Bill ran into the kitchen, grabbed a towel, and gently wrapped it around our daughter's head. Then we sped off to the hospital, praying all the way.

The doctor sewed up the forehead wound, which turned out to be the only injury. When we returned home, grateful that we still had a beautiful child to love, the kitchen floor was immaculate— no blood, glass, or pop spills. Bill called the women of the church to thank them for cleaning up the mess. My heart swelled with gratitude for this outpouring of love for our family.

Chapter Three

Bill

1

THE TWO SMALLER CHURCHES of my parish in Logansport, Indiana—Lucerne and Concord—had so few members, a committee was formed to vote on whether to unite them into one. The churches were only a few miles apart. And cutting down the number of services I had to present every week certainly appealed to me. But many members of both congregations believed the churches should remain separate.

At the reorganization meeting, after several minutes of rather heated debate, one of the pillars of the Lucerne church, Marge Burroughs, said, "This is probably a silly idea, and you all probably won't like it." She took a long, deep breath, as if to steel her nerves. "But what if we sold our church and let the town turn it into a community building for the kids."

After talking about the potential problems, and the advantages, we all decided the idea just might work.

During the official uniting service, I had trouble suppressing tears of relief and joy. This was the first time I showed those emotions during a public worship service.

2

Four months later, the presbytery named me director of a one-week, statewide summer youth conference. My parents offered to come and stay with two-year-old Becky so Jo and I could go together. The morning after we returned from the conference, the three of us would leave for a vacation in the Upper Peninsula of Michigan.

I spent two very busy months preparing for Camp Kosciusko. During the camp, everything I did worked out perfectly. I seemed to be much quicker and more intelligent than everyone else there. On the last night of the conference, during the recreation period, I won a game of checkers in record time. I felt undefeatable, serene, and powerful.

That night, a dust storm of anxiety swirled through my insides all night long. The next morning, I left the camp feeling confused and frightened. But once I was on the road, I felt in charge of everything. The earth, the sun, and the sky were mine, as if I'd been the one who had made all of it happen.

I arrived home eight hours ahead of schedule. When I walked in the door, my parents stared at me with confused expressions. "Where's Jo?" Mom asked.

In my mixed-up state of euphoria, fear, and confusion, I had left camp without her.

Chapter Four

Jo

1

BILL HAD WORKED HARD to prepare for the conference, and by the time we arrived at camp, he was exhausted and on edge. A sense of uneasiness held me in its grip and hung on tenaciously throughout the week. I prayed for strength for both of us. Did others sense that something might be wrong?

On the last day of the conference, while campers and counselors prepared to leave, I looked for Bill but couldn't find him or the car. My heart raced. I asked other counselors if they had seen him. When someone said she thought she'd seen him drive away, I asked a woman I barely knew if she could take me home to Logansport.

The ride was painfully quiet as I struggled with dread of what might have happened to my husband. When I arrived home, the confused expression on Bill's face, and the worried look in his mother's eyes, told me something horrible had happened. But I was so thankful to find my husband safe at home, I didn't even ask for details.

Instead of taking the post-camp vacation we'd planned, Bill and I headed for the hospital in Cincinnati. Once again, Dr. Jacobson provided Bill with medication, rest, and psychotherapy. He released Bill after two and a half weeks.

For the next week, we lived at Bill's parents' cottage in Kentucky. He spent the time praying, reading, fishing, and connecting with his family. I appreciated the respite from our busy pastorate life. Bill's mother made nutritious meals and took loving care of Becky.

Because we had planned to be on vacation after camp, we assumed the church members were unaware of what had happened. When we returned to the parish, we once again became a contented family. Life settled into a comfortable groove for the next several months. Everything was going well at church. Attendance was way up, the two congregations had merged, the youth group was flourishing, and I enjoyed being loved and pampered by the parishioners. Yet I could sense that Bill was getting restless.

One day he confessed to me that the excitement of new challenges was gone. "I hate the thought of leaving these wonderful, caring people. But I believe my work here is coming to an end."

After giving it some thought, I agreed with him. I even got excited about us moving on up the ecclesiastical ladder! Bill sent a notice to churches across the country, informing them that he was available and ready for a move to a new position.

At 7:00 one Sunday morning in early March, Bill got a call from the head of a pulpit committee in Marion, Indiana. They were coming that morning to hear Bill preach, and they planned to stop by the house after the service to interview us.

After he hung up, I asked, "Why did they call at the last minute?"

"I don't know. But you'd better get the place in shape while I go over my sermon one more time."

Inwardly I grumbled. They'd probably want to see the whole house. Most of it was in pretty good shape, especially the living room, which I usually managed to keep tidy enough for drop-in visitors. But I didn't bother doing that with our bedroom. We'd strewn clothes everywhere when we got ready for church that morning. I threw stuff under the bed and into the closet. Becky came in and offered to help, so I instructed her to scoop up my underwear and place it in her small wicker clothes hamper.

I knew nothing about the church in Marion, Indiana. But this might be our golden opportunity to move to a larger church. I wanted the pulpit committee to be pleased with Bill and with me and our home.

Bill hurried out the door early, hoping to meet the pulpit committee before service started. A few minutes later, I picked up Becky and headed outside. It was a beautiful, sunny day. The short walk between our house and the church fueled my excitement as I thought about being able to show off my little family. I lingered in the foyer until a few minutes before service started, then took my seat. Moments later, six people dressed in city clothes came in and took seats in the back of the church. (So much for my hope of making a good first impression on the committee.)

The service went well, and I marveled again at my gifted husband's preaching. As usual, his sermon came alive with God's Spirit. And Becky sat quietly in the pew beside me with her coloring books, pausing at times to smile up at me.

After the service, the usual parishioners flocked around me and my daughter, wanting to chat and hold Becky. My little girl soaked up all the attention. From the corner of my eye, I saw Bill greet the pulpit committee, then take off in the direction of our home. When Becky and I neared the house, I heard loud chatter through the open window, followed by a burst of laughter.

Sounds like they're already feeling comfortable. I breathed a sigh of relief.

When I opened the front door, Becky ran to greet her father. He picked her up and gave her a warm hug. Everyone else stood, and Bill introduced me to the six committee members. "Now that my wife is here," he said, "would you like a tour of our home?"

As we took our guests through each room, I was thankful I'd at least had time to pick up a bit before church. After the tour, our visitors settled in the living room. Following a short period of chitchat, the serious conversation began.

"What is your statement of faith?"

"What is your philosophy of how to minister to a congregation?"

The questions seemed endless. Bill answered them well. I felt proud of him.

Then it was my turn. They asked me questions like "What is the role of a pastor's wife?"

I had thought about all of their questions before, and I gave answers that I hoped sounded intelligent and sincere.

At one point, Becky decided to get some attention of her own. She marched across the living room and handed me something. Lost in my responses to our guests' questions, I accepted her treasure without even looking at it, nervously playing with it as I continued expounding on my point. Bill trying to get my attention, cleared his throat. Then coughed. Then ran his fingers across his forehead. Everyone else in the room seemed to be holding their breath. Eventually I looked down at my hands and realized that I'd been playing with one of my bras.

I gasped, muttered, "Excuse me," and stuffed the unmentionable into the magazine rack next to my chair. I kept speaking, despite some giggles and snickers. Finally, everyone in the room started laughing. Bill and I joined in.

My husband really wanted to go to Marion, and he was sure we would be invited, in spite of the bra incident. But somehow I knew that wouldn't happen.

And it didn't.

2

After we had been informed that we would not be invited to the pastorate of the Marion church, Bill informed the National Church that he was interested in assuming a new position. A few weeks later, letters started arriving from a number of churches, expressing their desire to talk with him.

One evening, the chairperson of the pulpit committee from a 600-member Presbyterian church in Warsaw, Indiana, called, stating that the committee would be coming to hear Bill preach at the Bethlehem church that coming Sunday.

I wondered what our members thought when they saw a large group of new people in the congregation. Did they know it was a pulpit nominating committee?

After the service, the chairman invited Bill to come to their church for an interview. A few weeks later, they called to invite him to become their pastor. God had answered our prayers for direction!

Every congregation has its own persona. Some are friendly, others more formal. The lay leadership may be strong, or the pastor might do all the work. The attendees may be characterized as conservative or liberal.

The Warsaw church had very traditional members. Bill and I were well grounded in our faith, but he was full of new ideas and impatient for change. I felt we were mismatched for this church. But Bill was energized by the challenge of serving a large church with many diverse people and theological positions.

When the church's trustee showed us the rental home where we would be staying, I couldn't hide my disappointment. The entire house was painted dark green, inside and out. Must have been a sale on green paint that month. The floors were covered with shabby linoleum, and the screen in the back door was torn. One of the two bedrooms looked more like an attic, accessible only by a narrow stairway.

Seeing our disappointment, the trustee assured us that, "until the church decides whether to remodel the manse or to give you a housing allowance, this is just a temporary arrangement."

But I wanted a comfortable, clean, inviting home for my family, especially since we were expecting another child soon.

During our first months in the Warsaw parish, a few people brought food over, but then we were left alone. No one invited us to dinner or to any cultural events. As we contemplated this, the reason seemed to become clear. Bill had told the pulpit nominating committee that his seminary professors taught that pastors and their wives should not make friends with their church members for fear of favoritism. After several years of isolation and loneliness, we had come to realize that this advice was wrong. But if we were going to make friends here, I would have to initiate those relationships.

I started by inviting the church officers and their wives over for dinner. After the meal, we played games. Both activities helped us to get to know and trust one another.

Three months after we arrived in Warsaw, I awoke one Saturday night in labor pains. Bill had to preach the next morning; he needed his sleep. I didn't want to chance another episode like the one in Logansport when Bill ended up in the psych ward. So I decided to get myself to the hospital.

I slipped out of bed and immediately doubled over with pain. Clamping my mouth shut to muffle an instinctive whimper, I grabbed the door frame to keep from falling to the floor. After recovering my balance, I scooped up my bathrobe from the side of the bed, inched my arms into the sleeves, then sat on the stair landing.

Again, my midsection throbbed. Unable to hold back, I cried out. But neither Bill nor Becky moved.

I slid from one step to the next like a baby learning to walk. With painfully slow progress, I made my way across the slippery kitchen floor to the muddy back porch, along the stone path, and up the cracked cement steps into the garage. On bare feet, I picked my way through the musty garage and strained to open the heavy door. Then I heaved myself behind the Plymouths steering wheel.

Market Street was empty. But I had no idea where the hospital was. My family has always laughed about my lack of a sense of direction. But it was not funny. I was alone in the dark and in pain.

I searched through town, driving up and down streets as if I were tracing a spider web. Finally, a brightly lit, yellow brick building appeared. I parked, then hobbled to the reception area. An ER nurse led me to a dim room, where I sat and listened to screams coming from down the hall. After a cursory examination, the doctor gave me a disappointing message: "False labor."

At four a.m., I drove home and went back to bed. As I rubbed my tummy, I smiled. At least Bill's sleep had been protected.

The following Saturday night, I went into labor again. But this time it happened at 11:00, before Bill and I retired for the night. I called a neighbor in to watch Becky, then Bill drove me to the hospital.

My labor continued for hours. At 3:30 in the morning, the doctor estimated we'd have to wait another eight hours or so. Since Bill had to deliver a sermon that morning, the doctor suggested he go home and get a little sleep. Reluctantly, my husband followed his advice.

The doctor's estimate was a few hours off. Jeffrey Allen Vamos was born at 8:30 a.m. He arrived so quickly there was no way to let Bill know in time for him to rush to the hospital. But I didn't resent his absence, knowing he had an important job of preaching for two services that morning—including one that started at 9:00.

Bill had asked one of the church officers to sit in the back row of the sanctuary, and if the baby arrived while he preached, he was to put up one finger if it was a girl and two for a boy. As Bill was making the third point in his sermon, up went two fingers. Bill paused for a second, then finished the sermon.

Later, Bill told me he had no idea what he said after that moment. But a number of folks assured him that he had delivered a powerful sermon.

3

Unlike Becky, who slept through the night from the day she came home, Jeffrey napped during the day and stayed awake all night. I spent many hours rocking him in an old wooden rocker, refinished for us by a member of the Bethlehem church in Logansport. Some nights, as I softly sang him to sleep, caressing his tiny face, I didn't want those peaceful moments to end.

As I cuddled him in my arms, I wished I could simply enjoy my children and let Bill handle the church affairs. But I knew I would soon need to resume my responsibilities as a pastor's wife.

When no one came forward to work with the youth group at the church, Bill asked me if I'd do it. I should have known better. With the sleep deprivation of new motherhood, my life was already challenging. But I had worked with the youth group at our last church, and it had been great. Besides, my husband and my church needed me. How could I say no?

Unlike the youth group that had changed Bill's life when he was a sophomore in high school, this group was led by a bully named Mary. Most of the others followed her lead for fear she might make fun of them. Our Sunday night meetings began with prayer, often interrupted by Mary's giggling. I would ask one of the teens to read a Bible passage, and if he stumbled over a word, Mary and her cohorts made fun of him. They distracted guest speakers by engaging in whispered conversations.

My anger came out in tears of frustration as I wondered whether I was accomplishing anything good with that group. After six months of agony, as Bill was reading the newspaper one

Sunday night, I ran through the back door, sobbing, went straight to our bedroom, and threw myself on the bed.

Bill came in right behind me. "What's wrong?"

"Two of the kids told me I'm too sensitive to work with the senior high students. I asked if I should quit. And Mary said yes!"

"What did you do?"

"What else could I do?" I shouted. "I quit!" After investing so much time and energy into this ministry, I felt hurt, betrayed, as if my heart had been seared with a branding iron.

Bill sat on the edge of the bed. "Why would they think you're too sensitive?" he asked softly.

"When I showed a movie about infants starving in India, I teared up."

Bill shook his head. "I'm going to call Mary."

I glared at him. "Don't you dare."

"I'm sure she'll apologize."

I doubted that. But Bill called anyway. He held the phone a little distance from his ear so I could hear the conversation.

"Mary," he said, "Jo tells me you guys had a little misunderstanding tonight. Sometimes things get tense in any group. Why don't we just forget the whole thing?"

"No," Mary responded in a firm voice. "It'd be better if she quit."

I dissolved into tears again. Bill's jaw clenched as he worked to control his anger. "Mary," he said calmly, "Jo led the youth group in our last church, and it flourished. We started with four kids and she grew it to fifteen. The students loved her."

No response.

"You owe her an apology, young lady."

Still nothing.

Bill's face reddened, and his hand gripped the phone as if he were trying to wrench Mary's apology out of the receiver. "Look, if you think you and your friends are going to get away with hurting my wife, you'd better think again."

Silence continued on the other end of the line. "This isn't over," Bill said, then hung up.

My heart pounded. "I told you that girl was nasty." I threw my arms around his neck and he caressed my hair. I knew, no matter what, I could count on this man's love. And that was more important than anything.

4

I dreaded going back to church after that. But, mercifully, Mary made herself scarce around me. A few weeks later, another parent offered to take charge of the youth group, and I gladly relinquished my position to her.

I never heard from Mary's parents and had no idea where they stood. But after several weeks of processing the experience, I got together with the mother of two boys in the youth group and told her what had happened, from my perspective. "You had every right to say and do whatever you needed to say and do," she told me. "I never take my boys' side against a teacher, because it causes them to lose respect for authority."

How wise.

She gazed at me with compassion. "Jo, I don't think you realize how much you got through to those kids."

Her words provided a powerful healing for my heart.

5

A year after we moved to Warsaw, the trustees of the church gave us a housing allowance so we could buy our own home. I was ecstatic!

As we started our search, I looked for something that would resemble the home of my early childhood, a stately old house that stood on a shaded, tree-lined street on the edge of the campus in Wooster, Ohio. Its exterior was stark white, with a wraparound porch.

Amazingly, a recently restored white-frame home on Main Street became available. Perfect! We bought it.

But living on a big thoroughfare presented certain challenges. One evening when I came home from a women's association meeting, sunlight flickered on the stark front porch, devoid of anything but one lone light bulb in the ceiling. We couldn't afford patio furniture. But perhaps exchanging the colorless bulb for a brightly colored one would make a difference. I put in a pretty crimson bulb and was delighted with the simple transformation.

A few weeks later, as I was making dinner, the doorbell rang. I ran to the door, hair in curlers, wearing an apron with a lighthouse printed on the front. I opened the door and saw a well-dressed man. His smile froze when he saw me. He shifted his weight while mumbling something about a person he was looking for. Then he excused himself and hurried away.

After I closed the door, I wondered why this stranger had knocked on our door. Then it hit me. The new porch bulb was red. Did he think this was the "red light district"?

6

My mother often told me that if a preacher had one good sermon a month he was doing well. Bill seldom had a bad sermon. Each was well researched and constructed, always including a story to bring the point home. Even his titles were interesting: "Gossip, Guilt, and God," "The Ministry of Christmas Shopping," "If I Were in Your Shoes." When his sermon was controversial, he stood tall and took a stand for God and against injustice. Every Sunday morning, his hard work and the Holy Spirit became partners.

Sometimes, on Saturday night, Bill asked me to listen to his sermon. Having heard many sermons over the years, I expected some to fall flat. Occasionally, after he had finished his practice run, I thought, *That was pretty awful.* But I couldn't tell Bill that. After all, it was already Saturday night. He didn't have time to make major changes. But on Sunday morning, his sermon came alive. I believe the energy of the people and the power of the Holy Spirit, combined with Bill's charismatic personality, made the difference.

Chapter Five

Bill

1

WHEN I ANNOUNCED MY SERMON SUBJECT for the upcoming Sunday, "The Healing of Racial Prejudice," a shiver coursed through my body. How could I speak on such a sensitive subject without offending some of my parishioners? I regretted telling them a week in advance. Now I was stuck with it.

At the time, Martin Luther King and other black leaders in the South were trying to raise people's awareness about unequal treatment of African Americans in jobs, housing, and voting rights. The congregation was used to my preaching on controversial issues. But this sermon would have to be the equivalent of a no-hitter in baseball or a perfect 300 game in bowling.

On Saturday night, around 11:20, the sermon was still shaky. And so was I. I asked Jo if I could try it out on her. When I finished, I said, "This is bad, isn't it?"

"It's a good sermon, one of your best," she said. "You're just tired. I know you'll do well. You always do." She smiled, kissed my forehead, and gave me a hug.

Early the next morning, I practiced my sermon one more time. Every minute or two, I stopped for a few seconds and prayed.

When I approached the podium to preach, I felt peace, even though I knew the sermon would not be easy for my parishioners to hear.

"In Galatians 3:28, Paul writes, 'There is neither Jew nor Greek, there is neither slave nor free, there is neither male nor female: for you all are one in Christ Jesus.' Prejudice is a neurotic sickness. It is the disease of insecurity. We put people down because we don't like ourselves, as though downgrading others will raise us higher. Paul says Jesus made everybody equal."

As I reminded them of the importance of seeing all men as Christ sees them, my parishioners seemed to be listening attentively. But I wondered if my words were getting through. So, I made it personal. "What if, when you looked in the mirror tomorrow morning, your skin was black? Would you be a different person?" A hush fell over the sanctuary. "We can be healed of prejudice by seeing every person, including ourselves, as someone for whom Jesus died."

As I left the platform, I felt exhilarated. You *did a great job, Bill. That was terrific!* But on the drive home, Jo railed at me. "The congregation didn't like your sermon today."

"What makes you think that?" I asked, perplexed.

"Not one person spoke to me after church."

"Maybe folks were just in a hurry to spend the day with family and friends."

"You only see what you want to see."

I had no idea why Jo was so upset.

We would win this spiritual battle. But I wanted my wife to be on my side instead of being another battlefront.

Jo

I didn't understand why I felt so unhappy in our new church, why I felt like I just didn't fit in. Or what to do about it.

After church one Sunday, as folks were leaving, the women I'd thought were my friends again left the sanctuary without speaking to me, or even making eye contact. What had I done to make them treat me this way?

I stood in a corner of the foyer, holding back tears as I watched these women chatting, with their backs turned to me. A gentleman from the congregation came up to me and whispered, "I know why those old biddies don't like you. It's because you're too sexy."

I laughed out loud, then walked out the door without a backward glance at the "old biddies."

Bill

Between sermons, counseling, and caring for our growing family, I carried a pretty heavy load. But I found my responsibilities quite rewarding. A favorite part of my work was counseling my church members.

I'd had some training in seminary on the fundamentals of counseling, but my best preparation came through my own suffering. In God's great wisdom, He enabled me to experience things that gave me the kind of insight that comes only from firsthand experience.

Ellen was one of the congregants I counseled. One year after my family and I moved to Warsaw, she walked into my study at the church. Six months earlier, when I called on her family to see if she'd like to attend our church, she had been the picture of confidence. But that day in my office, I could tell she was in pain. She shuffled through the open doorway and collapsed into the chair opposite my desk. Her eyes were red and puffy, and she looked restless and lost.

"I don't know if you remember me," she said quietly.

"Of course I do. I very much enjoyed meeting you and your husband in your home." I was disappointed that they hadn't accepted my invitation to visit our church, but I understood that it sometimes takes people a while to warm up to the idea. And that some people just don't have any interest in attending church—especially one with a prophetic preacher.

"When you called on us, you didn't push us about coming to church. It was like you'd just stopped by to meet us, with no strings attached."

"That was my intention. I'm glad you saw it that way."

She fumbled with a crumpled-up tissue. "I'm sorry to intrude, but I needed to talk to someone, and for some reason I feel like I can trust you."

I nodded and waited for her to continue.

"I used to be a social drinker. But beer became irresistible to me. When I drank, I felt free to say things I was normally afraid to express. The alcohol loosened me up. Only when I drank did I feel like myself."

God, I prayed, *help me to help her.*

"My husband got upset with my drinking, so I started going to bars at night, often not coming home until three or four in the morning. Tom got very angry about that."

I wondered how he expressed that anger but didn't want to press her for details. If she came in for later counseling sessions, we could discuss that issue.

"Lately I've been feeling tremendous guilt." She started sobbing. "I can't even look in a mirror because I don't want to see myself. I just want to run away from everything. To lock myself up someplace where guilt can't find me and choke me." She looked up. "Reverend Vamos, can you help me escape myself?"

I'd had the same thoughts when I was in the hospital after my breakdown. But I knew that if God could help me, He could help Ellen too. "Have you ever thought of asking God to forgive you?" I asked gently.

"God wouldn't accept a drunk like me," she murmured.

"Actually, you're just the kind of person God especially loves. The only people Jesus didn't forgive are those who thought they were too good to be forgiven."

She said nothing, but I could tell my words had reached her heart. For the first time since she had dragged herself into my office, her shoulders relaxed a little.

"Jesus is reaching out to you, no matter what you've done or how you feel. You can try to shove Him away, but He won't leave." These were not just hollow words. I had learned this truth many times, especially when I was ill.

"Are you sure He hasn't grown tired of my stupid failures and given up on me?"

God had stayed by my side through the three episodes of hell I'd lived through. I knew He wouldn't give up on Ellen either. "Yes, I'm sure."

Tears streamed down her face. Ellen had been forgiven. But there was still work ahead; she needed to forgive herself. I asked, "Will you pray with me?"

"I'm not sure I know how to pray. But I'm willing to try."

Ellen moved her chair closer to my desk, and I bowed my head. For a moment, I couldn't think of anything to say. But the quiet seemed to do its own praying. Finally, words spilled out. "Lord, let Ellen know that she is forgiven."

Nothing else came. I felt totally inadequate, almost embarrassed. Surely a man of God would have more to say than that, especially at such a crucial moment. But my mind was blank. All I could say was "Amen."

Ellen raised tear-filled eyes toward me, but said nothing. She left my office, her face looking more relaxed than when she came in—even serene.

A week later, when she came in for her second appointment, Ellen looked like a child who'd just eaten a gingerbread cookie for the first time. "I am beginning to ask God to help me forgive myself," she announced triumphantly.

In my heart I rejoiced, but I knew the journey for Ellen was just beginning. During our session that day, we spent most of the time talking about forgiveness.

One month later, she came back to see me. "I stayed away from alcohol for weeks after our first meeting. I was sure I could have just one beer. Before I knew it, I'd downed a whole six-pack. A few days later, the same thing happened. My husband couldn't figure out how to get me to stop, so he moved all of our money to another bank, and he didn't put my name on the account."

I was glad she had come to me, even after her disappointments and failures. It was evidence that she knew I still accepted her and that God loved her. I told her about Alcoholics Anonymous and made her promise she would attend their meetings. "You're not alone in this," I assured her. "I want you to come in to see me once a week. And you can call me anytime you're tempted to take a drink."

Ellen got up from her chair, knelt beside my desk, and asked for prayer. I put my hands over hers. "Lord, You know that Ellen is struggling with a drinking problem. Please take away her desire for alcohol. Amen." It was a simple prayer, but I didn't want to preach to her in prayer.

Before she left, I encouraged her to pray on her own.

"I'm willing to try anything."

Ellen attended the AA meetings faithfully. She learned a lot about herself and realized that her body chemistry didn't tolerate alcohol. That was why she couldn't stop drinking after just one or two beers. AA gave her tools for recovery.

Her weekly visits to my office were another powerful part of her healing. After struggling for months with self-hatred, she finally began to believe that she could forgive herself.

In time, Ellen became confident and strong, an inspiration to everyone who knew her. She is living proof of the power of God's compassion, grace, and mercy.

Chapter Six

Jo

1

I admired Bill's prophetic preaching, his strong stand against injustice, and his compassion for people. But he did not walk the journey alone; God was his support. He could also count on me.

And yet, there were times when I was reluctant to admit that Bill was my husband. He became a controversial figure in the community. Although he was loved, admired, and respected by most people in the church and community, some didn't even think he was a Christian. A few folks told him they believed he was going to hell for being what they called "a nigger-loving commie."

Bill was too busy to let such things bother him, but those comments hurt me. I wanted everyone to love my husband.

One Monday morning in August, I stopped by the drugstore to pick up some vitamins for baby Jeff. My neighbor Sara tapped me on the shoulder. "I see your lights on around six-thirty every morning. Why do you get up so early?"

"It's my husband who rises at dawn every day," I said, feeling defensive.

"I thought pastors worked only one day a week."

I cringed at the common misconception. "Yes," I said. "On Sundays he preaches. The other days he studies Scripture, prepares his sermons, and goes over them a number of times. But he has meetings almost every night: with the trustees, with the ruling body of the church, with the worship committee, evangelism meetings, new member meetings, stewardship meetings, Christian education meetings." After pausing to catch my breath, I said, "He also calls on all of our church members. And we have more than six hundred."

She stared at me in disbelief.

"He also conducts weddings and funerals, and does counseling with those who need it. In addition, he makes time to spend with the family." I sighed. "But even our vacations are often interrupted by his work. This past summer, we planned a little trip to a fishing village in the Upper Peninsula of Michigan. As we were about to walk out the door, the phone rang, and the funeral director told Bill that one of our church members had killed himself. We had to cancel our vacation so Bill could conduct the funeral."

"I never realized."

I suspect she regretted asking me about the early-morning lights. But I reveled in a sense of satisfaction that at least one other person knew the truth about a pastor's "easy" life.

2

Every August, Bill and I and the children spent two weeks in Cedarville, Michigan, with his parents. Bill looked forward to the fishing. I enjoyed every moment of our time away, even the long drive from Indiana to the Upper Peninsula, filled with happy talk and sack lunches.

Life in Cedarville was a reminder of a simpler time. We stayed in log cabins overlooking Lake Huron. Coffee brewed in an old tin pot on the stove. We ate homemade *kuchen* and fresh fish. Relaxed in a huge motorized fishing boat. Read novels. Took afternoon naps followed by more fishing until the sun retreated beyond the horizon.

Chapter Seven

Bill

1

I loved Jo so much, I would move mountains to keep her happy. But four years after we moved to Warsaw, that strange "insulated high" sensation started dominating my life again. People, buildings, sky, and clouds all had intense color and depth, as though I were looking at everything through a microscope. I felt I had brick-wall safety and a mountaintop view of life.

But that blue-sky euphoria only stayed with me for a few weeks, replaced by pounding, scraping anxiety.

My presbytery elected me and five other pastors to attend our annual general assembly, the highest ruling body of our denomination—like the House of Representatives, the Senate, and the Supreme Court all rolled into one ten-day pressure cooker.

My parents offered to watch the kids. I was thankful my wife would be able to join me.

I had a month to prepare. Night after night, I pored over the preparatory materials stacked in two-foot piles around my recliner. Even as I read, I was thinking about all my other work that wasn't getting done. Blaring messages raced around my mind, bumping into one another. *You'll never finish. Gotta read that new creed. I missed my hospital call on Mr. Johnson today. I'm behind on my sermon. Slow down. Hurry up. Can't think.*

I grew accustomed to wide-eyed nights and anxious nineteen-hour days. Jo was proud of me for everything I accomplished. But rancid anxiety haunted me.

At the general assembly, I felt buried under an avalanche of brilliant, poignant, and boring speeches, sore elbows, a throbbing tailbone, greasy-spoon lunches, and a five-foot-six, apple-cheeked guy from Whitewater Valley Presbytery who kept saying, "Point of order, Mr. Moderator," whenever the rest of us were ready to vote.

I took sleeping pills every night, but I still awakened in the wee hours and paced, worrying out loud. Jo's hugs and patience sustained me.

On the last day, the senior member of our delegation said, "Bill, I want to congratulate you on the way you conducted yourself this week. Your perspective is always clear and focused."

I couldn't say a word as I shook his hand, so grateful that I'd made it through the assembly without a breakdown, and that no one suspected my turmoil. But back home, I remained sleepless. After losing nine pounds in two weeks, I called my doctor. He recommended I admit myself to the psych ward at the Good Samaritan Hospital in Cincinnati.

2

After I checked in at Good Samaritan, a nurse named Winnie had me change into a hospital gown, then set me in a chair and wrapped a rubber strap around my upper arm. "This will only hurt for a second," she said, preparing a needle. "Just a little pinprick."

After the injection, Winnie took me to a room with plain gray walls and dark gray wall-to-wall carpet. The white acoustical-tile ceiling had a panel missing. Three of the four beds had patients lying on them, one of whom was sound asleep. A couple of hard wooden chairs sat near the door, presumably for visitors. Small dressers held get-well cards and boxes of candy.

"Better get into bed, Bill. You'll be asleep soon." Her voice was tender, as though she understood my fear and confusion.

After gently patting my shoulder, she walked out the door. Suddenly, the room felt like a cavern in the bottom of a coal mine. The absolute quiet terrified me. None of the other three patients was even snoring.

What if I lose touch with reality and never come back? What if the shot doesn't work? Are my wife and kids OK? What if I never get out of here? I'm thirsty. Wish I had some orange juice. What if I never get well? What if I'm already psychotic?

The questions zoomed through my brain and hammered at my heart. Feeling woozy, I slipped into the only unoccupied bed. Fear ran through my body. I was so filled with anxiety that I couldn't move a muscle.

A narrow shaft of light crept under the door. The door opened, and the light grew brighter. The glowing beam of a flashlight poured over each of my fellow patients and then focused on me.

"Still not sleepy, Bill?" Winnie's soft voice invaded my fortress of fear. She came to my bed and took my hand. "Do you want to talk?"

I swallowed hard, then garbled out the most painful words I had ever spoken. "Please tell me I won't be crazy in the morning."

Winnie smiled. "None of my patients ever goes crazy. I refuse to let that happen."

I talked with Winnie for a good half hour. Slowly my body accepted the caressing calmness of sleep.

When I awakened the next morning, Winnie was giving the orders of the day to the other three men in my room. I felt glued to the bed, held fast by the heavy sleeping drug.

After my bunk mates left, Winnie slipped over to my bedside. "I told you that you wouldn't go crazy. Breakfast's in ten minutes."

"I'm not hungry," I moaned.

"See you in the dining room." The words floated over Winnie's shoulder as she walked out the door.

The swirling thoughts inside my head, mixed with the sleeping medicine, gave me a headache. The sharp pain felt like a steel bar pressing into my forehead. *I'm definitely not going to breakfast.*

Something smelled delicious. My rumbling stomach reminded me I hadn't eaten in days.

If I do go to the dining room, I'll sit in a corner all by myself.

The irresistible aromas sent invitations to every part of my body.

What if they won't let me sit by myself?

The smell of coffee filled my room.

What the heck. I can come back to my room if I have to.

I reached the dining room just as everyone had started to eat. I edged over to a food cart and, to my surprise, discovered a tray with my name on it. This was no mistake. I really was in a hotel for mental cripples.

I found a spot by the window. With my back to the dining room, I stared at the heavy December clouds and picked at my breakfast. I knew everyone else in the room was watching me, but I didn't turn around to look at them. My eyes began to burn and water. *Somebody in here is smoking!* I couldn't understand how anybody could smoke and eat at the same time.

Someone started rapping an eating utensil on the table—two short raps and one long, two short and one long. It irritated me so much I could hardly breathe.

"Just be thankful you don't have to take those rotten shock treatments every mornin' at six," a tired voice droned.

I kept my eyes riveted on the murky clouds. *Oh, God, get me out of here. I hate this place. Can't I be kooky in a nicer environment?*

"Would you like some more coffee?" Winnie filled my cup. "You haven't eaten much of your breakfast."

I shrugged, barely glancing up at her.

She gave me a quick wink, then headed for the heavy metal door and opened it. "Gotta go now. My shift's over. See you all tonight." She took a heavy ring of keys out of her uniform pocket and left the room. After the door closed, I heard a heavy click.

I'm locked in now. I can't get out of this jail for emotional cripples!

A shrill, inhuman shriek came from the middle of the dining room, followed by a loud, frenzied rapping and the sound of plastic plates and glasses crashing against the hard wood floor. I spun around and saw an old woman in a hospital gown, her dirty gray hair hanging down her deeply lined face, carrying a tray with the remains of her breakfast. She shouted obscenities as she repeatedly banged the end of her cane against the floor.

"Aw, shut up, Grandma," grumbled a small man with a large sign hanging around his neck that read *Charlie*. "Just 'cause you're older than us, that don't give you the right to blow your top."

A thin, bald man coughed, holding his hand over his mouth. A dark-haired woman wearing a tattered beige robe stared at her slippers, not moving, not even blinking.

My hand trembled so much my coffee sloshed over the sides of my cup. I turned back to the window. *God, I'll never make it in here. I'd rather die.*

But what about Jo? And the kids? If I died in a loony bin, would they ever get over it?

Did anyone else have a key to that big metal door?

The old woman's ugly epithets stopped. She shouted, "I want my blue dress," over and over again.

"Knock it off, Grandma," Charlie yelled. "You don't have a blue dress and you know it."

A young teenage girl in pink slippers came to the gray-haired woman's side, put her arm around her shoulders, and leaned in close. "My name's Jill. I'll help you find your dress."

"I tell ya, there ain't no blue dress." Charlie pounded his fist on the table. "All she's got is that hospital gown she's wearing."

"Where do you think your dress might be?" Jill asked her.

"No sense in looking." Grandma cracked her cane on the table. "It's gone. Some dirty, stinkin' thief stole it. Wait'll I catch the lousy—"

"Do you think they hid it someplace?"

"If they did and I find out, it'll be all-out war." The cane rocked the table.

"Maybe we can find their hiding place. Come with me and we'll look."

Grandma's gaze concentrated on the tip of her cane. Jill didn't move. Seeing them standing there like human statues filled me with panic. "Somebody do something!"

Grandma smacked the floor with the tip of her cane. "Let's go find the rat who took my dress!"

Jill took her hand and led her around the dining room, checking under each table. A couple of times Jill got down on her hands and knees to look into a corner. When they came to a tall, overloaded trash can, Grandma laid aside her cane and jammed her hands into the pile of junk, tossing the contents in all directions. Milk cartons, cigarette butts, pop cans, plastic cups, and other rubble bounced off the floor.

The pounding in my heart intensified. I held my hands over my ears and laid my face on the tabletop.

Jill quietly retrieved Grandma's discarded pieces of junk and stacked them on the tables. When the trash can was empty, Grandma stood and shouted, "Ain't here. Let's keep looking." She retrieved her cane and resumed her slow, determined walk.

They headed for my table. I jammed a bit of toast into my mouth and chewed as fast and hard as I could.

"Have you seen my blue dress?" Grandma asked.

I shook my head and looked away. To my relief, they went on their way to continue their treasure hunt elsewhere. When they neared the corner of the dining room nearest me, Grandma stopped and looked out the window. She tilted her head and gazed at the city, eight floors below. Her face became stiff and hard, with deep, craggy ruts, and her eyes glazed over with sadness.

"Please turn around." Jill's voice echoed with compassion. Grandma turned to face her. The young girl threw her arms around the old lady, hugging her tightly. A steady stream of tears rolled down the woman's face.

Grandma encircled Jill in an embrace. "I don't have a blue dress. Haven't had one for years." She dropped her cane and leaned hard on Jill.

My heart raced. Was this the future in store for me?

Chapter Eight

Jo

1

WHILE BILL WAS IN THE HOSPITAL, the children and I again stayed with Bill's parents in Cincinnati. This time I had more responsibility, as I needed to take care of four-year-old Jeffrey and seven-year-old Becky. As always, Bill's mother and father extended great love and hospitality to all of us.

Though I had once harbored recriminations at them over never letting Bill express his anger, I came to love and admire my in-laws. They loved their son deeply, and that love had made Bill the warm and caring human being he was, in spite of a disease we were struggling to understand.

Bill's mother busied herself in the kitchen, which she considered her sanctuary. The room was always alive with the addictive smells of chicken-noodle soup and fresh-baked German pastries.

The woman lived for her family, and I loved her for it. Violet was a small woman, barely five feet, with graying hair and thin legs streaked with varicose veins. She seemed to have endless energy. My children adored her. They loved cuddling with her at bedtime, when she read to them until they fell asleep. Her care and attention to the kids afforded me a few moments for rest and prayer at the end of the day.

One evening, after saying good night to the children, I moved to the living room and curled up on the oversized green sofa. In the quiet, my surroundings seemed to fade away, like a dusty road disappearing in the hazy mist, while a hailstorm of thoughts about Bill and our future pounded my brain. In an attempt to calm my heart, I prayed.

Thank You, God, that my husband is in a safe place. Thank You for Bill's parents, my children, and my husband. He has been my champion, my protector, my cheerleader. I have learned to trust him and to love him dearly. I ask You for his healing.

Even though the future still felt uncertain, a sense of calm settled over me.

Thank You, God, for teaching me to trust You.

2

Even though Bill had been hospitalized with a severe episode, the doctor released him after just eleven days. I desperately hoped the roller-coaster ride was over and looked forward to traveling a level path for a change.

Back home in Warsaw, Bill's return to work was seamless, since we had reported "severe exhaustion" to the parish as their pastor's reason for the leave of absence.

Late one afternoon, I heard footsteps on the front porch, followed by the doorbell ringing. I opened the door to a woman with a bruised, puffy face and a black eye. I thought she must be a vagrant, wanting money or food. When she cried out, "Jo, it's Gretchen," I gasped in shock. Gretchen was a member of the church, and I'd met her at one of the woman's circles.

"What happened?" I asked.

"My husband did this." She flung her arms around me. I held her for a moment, then led her to the living room couch. I ran to the kitchen for a box of tissues but found only paper towels, which I apologetically handed her.

"I had to talk to someone, and I knew you would listen and you wouldn't tell." Stifling her sobs, she held up a shaking thumb and forefinger an inch apart. "I came this close to killing myself."

I wrapped my arms around her and waited for her to say what she needed to tell me.

She shared details of a brutal, abusive, controlling husband, whom she still loved. I didn't have any experience with the legal system, nor was I a trained counselor, but I could listen. And that was what she needed.

When she finished pouring out her story, I encouraged her to see Bill for counseling. She agreed, but asked if she could come back and talk to me again.

"Of course," I said. "You are always welcome here."

Bill referred her to a professional counselor who specialized in the kind of help she needed.

Gretchen was lonely, and I believed the best way I could help her was to become her friend. Knowing she loved to play bridge, I asked two women from the community if they would join us. The four of us played, off and on, for as long as Bill and I lived in Warsaw.

She never referred to her husband, which was fine since she was receiving professional help. I wanted to ask her how he was doing but felt that if she wanted me to know she would tell me.

As time went on, Gretchen blossomed into a confident, healthy woman.

3

On June 2, 1967, Bill and I had another baby. Susan was the spitting imagine of Jeff, except for being female. Her light brown hair with soft curls was the perfect frame for her alabaster face.

Before Susan was born, she kept me awake almost every night. That must have worn her out, because after she came into the world, she slept through the night right away. And she was unbelievably good during the day. She brought everyone in the family tremendous joy.

Taking care of a newborn gave me a reprieve from my busy life of speaking engagements, entertaining friends and church committees, singing solos and in the choir, teaching Sunday school, and social obligations in the community. However, there was no letup for Bill.

Chapter Nine

Bill

NINETEEN SIXTY-EIGHT was a year of vast social and political changes across the globe: The United States with its anti–Vietnam War protests and civil rights movement, protests and revolutions in Europe, and unrelenting famine in Africa.

On February 4, Martin Luther King Jr. spoke at Ebenezer Baptist Church in Atlanta. His speech contained what amounted to his own eulogy. Two months later, on April 4, King was shot and killed. His assassination sparked riots in major cities all over the country. Forty-six deaths were blamed on the riots.

Later that day, Robert F. Kennedy heard about the murder as he was about to give a speech in Indianapolis, Indiana. He delivered a powerful extemporaneous eulogy in which he pleaded with the audience to "tame the savageness of man and make gentle the life of this world."[1]

Two months later, on June 4, Robert Kennedy was shot.

In August, during demonstrations at the Democratic National Convention in Chicago, police beat some of the marchers unconscious. Hundreds were sent to the emergency room.

---

1 Robert F. Kennedy, Remarks on the Assassination of Martin Luther King, Jr., delivered April 4, 1968, Indianapolis, Indiana, quoting the English translation of a passage from *Agamemnon* by Greek playwright Aeschylus.

This year of historical upheaval was a time of chaos in our personal lives as well.

We had been in Warsaw for six years when the chairperson of a political party asked me to run for the school board. I considered it a great compliment and agreed to do so. When the word leaked out to the community, my life was swept into a tsunami of uncertainty.

On April 13, 1968, I got a visit from Reub Williams, the owner of the *Warsaw Times Union*. "Rev," he said, "you know you're in trouble, don't you?" Without waiting for an answer, he handed me a newspaper from a nearby small town and pointed to the lead article. It spoke of a man who presented "an imminent and present danger to our community by planning to bring blacks from Detroit to help the unemployed here in Warsaw. This man is Pastor Bill Vamos."

I stared at the words in disbelief. "Where on earth did they get that idea?"

"Do you remember Al Reque?"

"Of course. He used to be on the church board. What does he have to do with this?"

"Al found a memo you wrote to your church board a year ago, and he circulated it to all of the area newspapers. Then he called a meeting of ten businessmen and told them about your plans to invite minority folks from Chicago to help with the job shortage."

I'd written that memo to tell the ruling body of our church about an idea I had to address the unskilled job shortage in Warsaw. I thought the plan had merit, but no one else did, so I'd forgotten about it.

"Al is suggesting that you be removed from the church and possibly the community."

I was stunned. "I can't believe one of my own church members would do such a thing." He shrugged. "With Martin Luther King being killed and all those horrible riots going on, your plan to bring black folks here has people frightened."

"But that memo was written a year ago. And the idea was discarded."

"I'm glad to hear that." Reub stood to leave. "You know, I listen to you on the radio every Sunday." He gave me a half grin. "I disagree with almost everything you say. But Warsaw could use someone who stirs things up and keeps us on our toes. I love this town. I want you to stay."

I nearly wept with relief as I shook his hand and thanked him profusely.

When I told Jo about this encounter, she reacted with shock. "What are we going to do?"

"Nothing for now. Reub said to sit tight until he gets back to me."

Sit tight. Easier said than done.

Chapter Ten

Jo

1

THE FOLLOWING SATURDAY, we traveled to our little cottage on Lake Sechrist, about a half hour from Warsaw, for some fun and relaxing family time. Becky, age nine, Jeffrey, age six, and one-year-old Susan all loved the lake . . . and the quality time with their parents. Bill had taught the older children how to bait hooks, catch fish, and clean them. I got to cook whatever fish they caught.

Soon after we arrived at the cottage, Jeff grabbed his toy trucks and cars and headed for the old sandbox in the backyard. Becky went fishing at the end of the dock. With Susan content in her playpen nearby, Bill and I worked in the yard. Enjoying the earth, the water, the sun, and the clean air restored our wounded spirits.

Bill and I were relaxing on our lawn chairs and sipping iced tea when a car door slammed in the parking lot above the cottage, followed by the muffled voices of two men as they made their way down the steps leading to our front door. Their expressions did not look friendly.

"Who are they?" I whispered.

"The men who asked me to be on the school board," Bill whispered back.

After Bill introduced me, they asked if they could have some private time with him. I picked up Susan, slipped into the cottage, and started to prepare supper. But it was impossible to concentrate. I opened a large can of tomatoes before realizing I didn't need tomatoes for my recipe.

After a half hour that felt like an eternity, Bill came into the house, alone.

"What did they want?" I asked.

"They said they will kill me in the press if I don't print a retraction to that memo about bringing black folks in from Chicago."

I gasped. "I thought those men were on your side."

Bill's eyes filled with pain and sadness as he gazed out the door. "So did I. But like Charlie told me, people are fickle." He turned to me. "Looks like we're going to need some extra help from God on this one."

At midnight on April 17, a two-hour meeting took place that included some of the most influential men in the community, including Reub and Bill. Their purpose was to map out a strategy that would protect Bill from those folks who wanted him out of the community or off the school board. It was decided that Bill should call a board meeting of the church leaders to let them know what was going on. Other than that, he was not to do or say anything about this mess.

Bill was incredibly grateful to those prominent leaders in the community who supported him, possibly at the risk of their own reputations.

When Bill arrived at the meeting with the church leaders, he felt as if everyone was against him. He had won their respect through the years. But would they realize that he was a man of integrity who needed their understanding and support? Would they decide to stand with him? And if they did, could they withstand the criticism from the community?

The church leaders voted unanimously to support Bill in not printing a retraction of a memo that had been written a year ago.

A few days after that meeting, Bill received a letter from John, a church trustee who frequently differed with Bill, often contentiously. It said, "You and I have often disagreed, but I fully support you in your present circumstances. No one should ever be the victim of inflammatory reporting."

Every few days, something appeared in the newspaper about Bill or our family. To our relief, it wasn't always negative. One afternoon, as we were at a picnic celebrating a special event in the community, as well as our anniversary, a newspaper reporter showed up, no doubt hoping to pick up a few tidbits of information. The next day, in a fun section of the newspaper called "The Town's Talking," the columnist reported:

> Mrs. William Vamos was wearing a lovely corsage. She and her husband had another reason to celebrate: it was their 10th wedding anniversary. She confided to the group that her usually calm, matter-of-fact husband (minister of the Warsaw First Presbyterian Church) showed a state of nerves one day that she will always remember. It was on their wedding day!

These amusing tidbits seemed to be a way of informing the community that Bill had the support of the local paper.

Soon after that, Bill came home from work one day and said he had a great compliment for me. "I ran into Mrs. Petrie, the speech teacher." I had substituted for her a couple of years ago at the high school. "She said that one of the main reasons I'm as effective as I am in the community is because of you. She said many other people feel the same way."

"You're kidding." I hadn't done much in the community for a while because I felt I needed to keep the family in one piece.

Her comment came at a time in my life when I desperately needed a word of encouragement.

2

Over the next six months, our lives went back to normal. The memo forgotten, Bill was appointed to the school board. When the news broke, all the bigwigs in town called to congratulate him. There was only one person who wasn't happy about the news: the president of the school board. Bill took stands on several issues that the president didn't agree with. So the president disregarded every suggestion he made during the meetings.

As Bill and I were getting ready to take some vacation time, we heard rumors of problems with some of the teachers. There was also a concern that the principal of the high school wasn't doing his job. Resolving those issues was the responsibility of the board.

As a pastor's wife, I'd learned long ago the importance of not sharing confidential information. That was difficult in this situation because there was so much misinformation. I felt sure that if I could give folks the whole story, they would understand.

Amid all this chaos, we took our vacation. The night we got back, there was a school board meeting. Bill learned that in his absence, the entire school board had fallen apart. The superintendent had fired some of the teachers, and the high school principal had resigned. The board members had been besieged with 2:00 a.m. phone calls, hate mail, and letters to the editor.

Things had become so chaotic, the board was meeting every week instead of once a month. So far there had been no demonstrations, but there was concern that these might take place.

The only piece of good news was that the local newspaper stood behind the board.

Attendance at church had gone down when we were on vacation, which was typical. But some folks told us it happened because Bill was on that "evil" school board.

Bill believed in the superintendent, seeing him as a man of integrity. But people came up to me and asked, "How can your husband support a man like that?"

Bill's open relationship with the superintendent enabled the other board members to stand as a unit rather than going off on their own in different directions. Even the board president, who had opposed most of Bill's suggestions in the beginning, came to trust Bill and rely on him. They actually became friends.

3

In the midst of the school board tensions, I told Bill I wanted to participate in the annual Tri Kappa talent show, a fundraiser for the community. He encouraged me to try out. I asked if he would consider singing a duet with me. After thinking about it for a moment, he said, "Jo, I would do anything for you, even die for you. But I will not sing with you. It's too scary!"

For the next week, I kept asking. When he realized how much it would mean to me, he relented.

During rehearsals, we had many moments of shaky knees and spasms in the pits of our stomachs. But on the night of the talent show, the two of us stood on stage in the high school auditorium singing "Make Believe." In front of that huge crowd, we felt invincible as we sang this love song to each other. The crowd gave us loud and long applause.

For the next several weeks, I basked in the glory of the accolades we received. But Bill didn't have time in his busy schedule to savor the recognition. In addition to his heavy church load and his responsibilities on the school board, he had to make sure "Worship in the Round" was functioning smoothly.

"Worship in the Round," a ministry conceived by several local pastors, was a contemporary service held in the open-air Wagon Wheel Playhouse. It included drama, dance, and modern music. The community loved it, and over the summer, Worship in the Round grew in effectiveness and popularity, becoming an exciting venture in new and creative forms of Christian worship. But it required a massive amount of work for the pastors who were involved.

4

Even with Bill's busy schedule, our lives were going well—with one exception. Though the two of us agreed on issues like money, politics, religion, and raising our children, we experienced tension when it came to meeting each other's sexual needs.

Bill sometimes became aggressive in his demands for sex—a stark contrast to the gentle man I had come to know. And this frightened me. I lay awake many nights, trying to make sense of this. Was it my fault? What could I do differently? Did other couples have this much dissatisfaction in the bedroom? Whenever we tried to discuss the subject, we ended up arguing.

After a while, I realized that Bill often became sexually aggressive right before he needed to be hospitalized for a manic high. That scared me even more.

One week, Bill decided to preach a sermon with the title "What Is the Christian's Viewpoint toward Sex?" Was this for my benefit? Or was he trying to sort through this issue for himself the only way he knew how?

Perspiration gathered around my neck and chest as I sang in the choir before Bill preached. Some members of the congregation would feel uncomfortable, even threatened, by his views on this subject. Would today's sermon cross a boundary, causing people to stop listening or even walk out of the service? When we finished our last song, I wanted to run up to Bill and plead with him to reconsider, to preach about something else—anything else. But I quietly took my seat in the choir loft, sharing my thoughts only in silent prayer.

"Many people today wonder what the Christian viewpoint is toward sex," he began. My heart sank. "Many ministers avoid this question, especially from the pulpit. But the church must teach what the Bible has to say, and Scripture speaks extensively about this issue."

Convinced that everyone in the congregation was staring at me, I kept my eyes focused on Bill. His hands trembled slightly, but his voice was strong with conviction.

Halfway through his sermon, I gave in to curiosity about the reaction of our people. Without turning my head, I tried to scan the congregation with only my eyes. They were all still in their seats; no one had left. As a matter of fact, everyone seemed mesmerized. *Thank You, God.* Bill was handling this touchy topic with tremendous sensitivity. Maybe everything would be all right after all.

Following the service, as people shook Bill's hand on their way out of the sanctuary, most of the comments were positive. Some members even congratulated him on his courage!

The next Sunday, Mrs. Weber cornered me after the service. She attacked every aspect of the previous week's sermon, as well as Bill's ministry in general. Having risen very early that morning to get three children ready for church, then teaching Sunday school and singing in the choir, I was too exhausted for an encounter with a difficult church member. But I kept my mouth shut and let her rant on.

Pointing her finger at my face, she muttered, "I can't believe your husband would preach a sermon on such a private subject. It made me feel dirty."

"Then you must not have heard what Bill was saying," I said as sweetly as I could. "His whole point was that sex in marriage is a good thing."

Ignoring my comment, she continued to rattle on. I felt an impending loss of control, and my determination to be nice waned. Unable to take any more, I interrupted her and let loose with a torrent of angry words, ending with "I feel sorry for your husband."

She gasped, then stormed out the side door.

As I drove home, I wondered if I should tell Bill about my outburst. I didn't want to add to his worries, and I sure didn't want to make him angry. In ten years of ministry, I had never told anyone off. To be honest, I felt no guilt.

When I walked into the living room, Bill asked about my conversation with Mrs. Weber, so I told him everything.

To my surprise, he cheered. "That should have happened to her a long time ago."

The next day he sent me flowers with a note that read, "I'm proud of you!"

Amazingly, Mrs. Weber and her husband did not leave the church. But her personality remained sour.

Chapter Eleven

Bill

AFTER A YEAR AND A HALF SERVING THE CHURCH in Warsaw, I felt a strong need to improve communication among the church members. I started a new ministry called "dialogue groups." For two months I met weekly with eight group leaders for the purpose of study, prayer, and the honest sharing of personal needs. We discussed how to better hear what others were really saying rather than making assumptions based on our own ideas and experiences. The leaders applied what they learned in their groups and also taught the members how to listen to one other.

Many in the church found this ministry extremely helpful for their own lives as well as for the life of the church. It caught on so well, I had to fight my recurring battle with a euphoric feeling of limitless power! This time I kept my feet on the ground by spending time every day in prayer for the dialogue group leaders. That discipline helped me focus on compassion toward others. I hoped this would help avert another breakdown.

Still, I was concerned about that possibility, so I made an appointment with my doctor. He recommended that I admit myself to the Cincinnati Hospital for a complete physical. There an internist told me I had "spastic gastroenteralgia," otherwise known as a serious case of heartburn. "What you need most," he said, "is a good night's sleep."

To make sure I followed his advice, the doctor prescribed a sedative that knocked me out in seconds.

After a few days of rest, I felt refreshed and ready to get back to work.

Chapter Twelve

Jo

WITH EVERYTHING GOING ON in our lives and in the church, I marveled at Bill's staying power and wondered where it came from. What kept him from sliding into the depressive side of his disease? He never seemed to have a down day, whereas I had experienced several days when I could barely make myself get out of bed in the morning.

I began to carefully observe how he responded to stressful, upsetting circumstances. I became convinced that an active prayer life and journaling were what kept depression at bay. Rather than becoming mired in anger and sadness, Bill brought his feelings to God in prayer and wrote about them in his journal.

When I was little, my family prayed often—before meals, at bedtime, for safe travel, for the sick, for relatives. Prayer was like a shield protecting us from harm. It felt as normal as eating and sleeping, and it continued to be a constant companion in my adult life and in my marriage. But now, as I reached to the heavens for sustenance and strength, I felt as if God had given up on me. Or maybe I had given up on Him.

I was spiritually bleeding and raw from the many battles my husband and I had been through—from the struggles on the school board, to the late-night phone calls with someone shouting horrible profanities, to the critical folks who expected perfection from us, some not even considering us to be Christians. On top of all that, in the back of my mind, there was always a deep concern for Bill's health.

I needed encouragement. But no one seemed to care. Perhaps because no one knew. However, I didn't feel comfortable revealing to anyone my concerns about Bill's health, the school board, or those critical folks in the church. I didn't want to jeopardize Bill's ministry.

Chapter Thirteen

Bill

1

I CAME HOME FROM AN IMPORTANT MEETING one night and heard Jo crying from the upstairs bedroom. The children were asleep and I figured she needed some time to herself, so I decided to wait awhile before going up. I walked to the kitchen to grab a bite to eat. When Jo's cries got louder, I ran to the bedroom.

The second I entered, she exploded into a shouting rage. "Either leave me forever, or leave your phony church members. I hate living in your shadow. I hate your superficial congregations. They want absolute perfection—not from themselves or God, oh no. They want you and me to be Reverend and Mrs. Perfect. Well, you can go on playing their stupid game, but I'm out. I want to live my own life. You're going to have to choose between being a pastor and being my husband."

As I stood at the foot of the bed, I felt the heavens pressing down on me so hard I couldn't move. I clawed through my mind for comforting words to say to my wife. Everything seemed pitiful and pointless. I had to get away. I had to think. So instead of responding to Jo's tirade, I turned and shuffled downstairs, then collapsed into a living room chair. I closed my eyes and prayed. *Please, God, be merciful and help us!*

I sat in silence for a long time. The quiet prayer time helped calm my fears. When I opened my eyes, I noticed a framed photograph on the mantle. I stood and stepped closer, warmth radiating inside me. The picture was our family Christmas photo, with Becky age nine, Jeff six, and Susan one. Jo and I stood behind them. I couldn't recall the last time my wife looked so vivacious and alive. My mind flashed back to the first time I saw Jo at Camp Presmont. I remembered that precious time of fun and laughter.

I took the frame from the mantel, pressed it to my chest, and held it tight. *Will we ever have happy times again?* Tears trickled down my cheeks, something I hadn't experienced in a long time. I placed the picture back on the mantel and headed up the stairs.

When I entered the bedroom, I found Jo staring out the window. I walked up to her and said, "I love you." She flung her arms around me and sobbed, nestling her head on my shoulder. Then we fell into bed and clung to each other. We lay there in silence for several moments. Then I whispered, "It's no contest, Jo, none at all. I am willing to leave the pastorate, but I'm not willing to lose you."

Jo fell asleep soon after that. But I lay there for a long time, thinking about what had just happened. I knew I was making the right decision. I loved Jo and would never want to lose her. But I couldn't imagine quitting the pastorate. It wasn't just something I did for a living. Preaching was at the heart of my identity. I didn't know, or want, anything else.

Unable to calm myself, even with prayer, I slipped out of bed and downed two sleeping tablets.

2

Jo and I talked endlessly about what the next step for our lives would be. I wanted to make sure it was right for both of us.

After much discussion, we decided I should pursue becoming a clinical psychology counselor. I had to work extra-hard to keep up with my responsibilities at the church while studying for this new career.

Shortly after I enrolled in classes, Dr. Rice, from a church in Elkhart, Indiana, about an hour away from our home, called and asked if I might consider being their pastor. This was one of the largest churches in our presbytery, with around twelve hundred members, and it had an excellent reputation. Normally, I would have jumped at the chance. But I turned him down because of the decision Jo and I had made for me to leave the ministry.

About six months later, as I was preparing for the final exam, I received a letter from a congregation in Pittsburgh, asking if I might consider a senior pastor's position at their church. The letter said they believed my theology would be a good match for their church of two thousand members. They were even willing to fly me and my family out there to talk about it.

My heart leaped at the thought that such a large church was interested in me. But how could I even consider taking another preaching job after I'd agreed to leave the pastorate for her? Setting my excitement aside, I slipped the letter into the top drawer of my desk.

For the next week, I couldn't focus on anything but that offer. Unable to contain my enthusiasm any longer, I finally decided to tell Jo about it. When I sheepishly handed her the letter one evening after work, she surprised me by not blowing up. Instead, she calmly asking how this church got my information. There was no mention of that in the letter.

"I have no idea."

"What do you know about the church?"

I couldn't believe she was actually open to discussing this. "Only what it says in the letter." I grinned. "But they must have a big budget if they can afford to pay our airfare just to meet us."

"And they must be serious about wanting to consider you."

I swallowed hard. "What do you think?"

She gave me a warm smile. "I think I am very proud to be the wife of such a sought-after pastor." We both chuckled.

"If we're going to consider this," I said, "it's going to require some heavy-duty praying."

Jo grinned. "I'm okay with that."

I contacted the Pittsburgh church and told them my wife and I were considering their offer and praying about it. A few weeks later, after getting confirmation from God and Jo that I should pursue this, I made plane reservations.

The next day I received a letter from Dr. Rice in Elkhart, asking if by any chance I might have changed my mind about my availability for a pastorate. When I read the pamphlet that had come with the letter, describing Elkhart's community and the church, it felt right. But I had already started on the path to a life outside the pastorate. I wondered why these two opportunities had surfaced at this time. Jo and I spent many hours weighing our options and praying. After numerous conversations, we decided to see what both churches had to offer and trust God to lead us.

We flew to Pennsylvania. The church building was a large Gothic structure in the heart of downtown Pittsburgh. A member of the church board met us out front. He seemed pleasant enough, but he appeared rushed, as if he had deadlines to meet.

While he walked us through the building, he explained that most of the church members were busy, successful business folks. He also told us that the heavy wooden doors had to be padlocked every time someone entered or left the church during the week. He made the church sound more like a country club than a vibrant community of faith. He then told us that we would be living in an apartment near the downtown area.

Padlocked doors and living downtown didn't make us feel safe about bringing our growing family here. With children aged eleven, eight, and three, we wanted a safe neighborhood with grass and trees, where the kids could walk to school.

After the tour, Jo and I agreed that this was not the church for us. I politely declined their call.

Chapter Fourteen

Jo

1

O N A COOL, WINDY SUNDAY MORNING in March, all seventeen members of the Elkhart pulpit committee traveled to our Warsaw church to hear Bill preach. The sanctuary was packed. No one seemed to notice the newcomers dispersed throughout the congregation.

I was excited about this new possibility for our family, but I felt nervous for Bill. I winked at him as he began the sermon. My husband looked handsome and distinguished as he stood behind the pulpit in his navy-blue suit and maroon tie. His dark hair had grown thick and slightly wavy, and a well-trimmed beard accentuated his brown eyes.

His sermon title that day was "Let's Be Honest." As I sat there listening, I thought, *I love the way my husband is so honest about himself, admitting his own self-righteousness and other shortcomings.*

When the service was over, the committee left quietly, leaving us to wonder what they thought. But on the following Thursday they invited us to their church in Elkhart for an interview with the pulpit committee.

Elkhart was known as "The City with a Heart," for two reasons. The community had a dynamic spirit. And the American

Indians thought the island between the St. Joseph and Elkhart Rivers looked like an elk's heart. As we drove through downtown Elkhart on our way to the church, the place looked like any other boring Indiana town. Its main street boasted a movie theater, a Sears Roebuck, two gas stations, and a McDonald's.

But as we crossed the bridge overlooking the St. Joseph River, the Presbyterian church came into view in all its majestic, serene splendor. The cathedrals of Europe couldn't have enchanted me more. The entire front of the church was a wall of clear glass surrounded by Indiana limestone. On the north side, hidden behind a stained-glass window, stood the chapel. On the south side, a tall bell tower rose like a beacon overlooking the city.

The chairperson of the pulpit committee met us at the side door and directed us into the sanctuary. Sunlight streamed through the stained-glass windows that covered the entire front wall, casting sunbeams over the stone-tile floor and the soft cushions of the wooden pews. Everything in the sanctuary was built to accommodate the acoustics, and I wondered if the architect had worked closely with a musician. I could almost hear the singing of the choir amidst a room ablaze with sunshine.

After a few moments bathing in the beauty that surrounded us, the chairperson led us down the hall to the church parlor, where he said the committee was waiting for us. The parlor was gorgeous, with walls, carpet, and upholstered furniture in a soft pastel blue. I felt drawn to this stunning room as if it were inviting me in.

Seventeen people sat in comfortable-looking chairs around an oval table. The chairman introduced us to them. There were housewives, teachers, business magnates, PhDs. A doctor, a company president, the principal of the high school, and the superintendent of schools. I was impressed with the caliber of people assembled there. Yet I felt comfortable in their midst.

Once the pleasantries were out of the way, they began pelting Bill with questions.

"I hope you don't plan on making any major changes to our worship service. You need to leave it like it is. Why mess with a good thing?"

"I understand you've started a contemporary, creative worship service. How soon could you do something like that here?"

"We need a pastor who keeps this church moving into the community. Can we depend on you to do that?"

"Our congregation has problems: job pressures, faltering marriages, kids who are into drugs and sex and are failing in school. We need someone who will draw this congregation together, unify us, and love our members. How do you plan to accomplish that?"

These people represented a wide variety of positions, some of which seemed to have opposite goals. Bill answered every question with practical yet creative ideas. There was no self-importance in his demeanor, but an air of confidence about what he believed. When he talked about his vision for the church, the committee responded positively. They seemed eager to grow in their faith. And when he talked about how important it was that he be able to reach out to the community as part of the church's witness, they affirmed him.

Everyone was friendly and interesting, and I took an immediate liking to them. I wondered if these people were aware of Bill's medical history. But that didn't matter. I felt proud of this man of God I had the privilege of being married to.

One of the committee members, a tall, stately woman in her middle years, had an inner beauty that was reflected in her face and eyes. Her name was Dorothy Ransom, and her presence calmed me. Her in-depth questions indicated she was a woman of culture and education. Halfway through the meeting, she asked me, "How do you see your role as pastor's wife? What are your interests and gifts, and how would you use them?"

I replied with a question of my own. "What are your expectations of me?"

The committee responded with warmth and humor, encouraging me to pursue my own interests.

Really? Had I heard correctly? They didn't expect me to be perfect? I could be myself, explore who I was meant to be?

After the meeting ended, Dorothy drove Bill and me to the parsonage. It was a white-framed two-story house in a peaceful neighborhood, with a little lake nearby. Everything had been repainted, inside and out, making the house glisten. There were four bedrooms—what a luxury! The grade school was almost in the backyard, so the children could easily walk to school. I knew I could be happy in this home.

As we drove back to Warsaw, everything felt right. Bill needed a challenge, and the Elkhart folks were willing to give him that. They seemed to believe that I would also be important to the church and community, that I had gifts to share. Bill looked at me and took a deep breath. "Are you ready to give the pastorate another chance?"

"I believe I am," I answered immediately.

After several conversations and prayers, we decided to accept the offer. It seemed that God was not done with us yet in the work of His ministry.

2

Our move to Elkhart was vastly different from our move to Warsaw. The church members cleaned the parsonage for us. Bill's study got new furniture. The day we moved in, the congregation provided meals and babysitting. And they didn't forget us after move-in day. For the next month, we were invited out every night for dinner or a social gathering.

I quickly adjusted to our new life. I enrolled Becky and Jeff in grade school. Susan, our three-year-old, kept me joyfully busy. When the choir director learned that I could sing, he welcomed me as if he'd hit the jackpot. He had been missing a soprano for quite some time. He asked me to sing many solos, and I shared my musical gifts with delight.

Bill had wanted a challenge, and he got one. The church had an equal number of liberals and conservatives, and neither side felt they were being heard.

When Bill was a seminary student, he served a church that was split down the middle like this one. He went to the seminary counselor and poured out his story in a two-hour-long session. When he finished, the counselor leaned back in his chair, took a deep breath, and said, "The more contact I have with what goes on in churches, the more convinced I am that a pastor's chief task is to keep the saints from biting each other!"

That was Bill's first task at the Elkhart church. With so many diverse theological positions, he said it was like "taming an octopus." But he believed he could draw the congregation together. He knew his best platform for change was the pulpit. So he preached inclusiveness, reminding the congregation that the church doesn't need to be theologically exclusive. Neither conservatives nor liberals have the whole truth, he reminded them, but together they could discover a spirit of openness.

The congregation was hungry for change, so Bill initiated new ministries. He started with the dialogue groups that had worked so well in the Warsaw church. He followed this with Bible studies and neighborhood friendship groups to strengthen the spiritual lives of the people.

Bill also called personally on each family in the congregation. Unlike the early days in Logansport, when he considered such visits to be a waste of time, he actually enjoyed his pastoral visits. He was a good listener, and his compassion was contagious.

When the church members began to feel as though someone was listening to them, they started to listen to each other, and they soon found that they were able to trust one another. The church grew in numbers as well as in faith.

3

The ruling body of the church gave us the option of living in the parsonage or accepting an allowance with which to buy our own home. Though we enjoyed living in the manse, we could build up financial equity by investing in a home of our own. That would also give me a chance to apply my decorating skills.

We found a little Cape Cod house on the lake, about a half block from the children's school. It needed a lot of work. The house didn't even have a family room. But Bill and I decided we could add the extra room if we decided we needed it.

Bill's parents thought we were crazy to even consider moving from our lovely parsonage. They were also concerned that, in the chaos of remodeling, Bill wouldn't have a place to get adequate rest. But we were determined, and we bought the place.

I had great fun choosing new carpeting, wallpaper, and paint. During construction, Bill did his work at a bedside table, which he kept completely organized.

After the remodel was completed, everyone in the family, including Bill's parents, was delighted. When Bill's mother saw how happy we were in our beautiful new surroundings, she understood how satisfying owning our own home was for us.

A year after our move to Elkhart, she died of a massive heart attack. Bill's mother had had a profound influence on him. Her deep faith and spirit of caring instilled in him a respect and empathy for others. This was most apparent in how he raised his children and in his ministries beyond the church. To this day, I miss her love, her acceptance.

Chapter Fifteen

Bill

ONE HUMID DAY IN AUGUST 1972, as I was working in my office at the church, I heard a loud rapping at the door. In bounced John, a high school science teacher from the congregation.

He started talking without sitting down. "Bill, federal funds have been cut off for those blighted areas that were being redeveloped in our city. It's outrageous! Something needs to be done. Do you think the church can help?"

"Perhaps. Why don't you sit down so we can talk about it?"

John spent the next half hour bemoaning the fact that, without financial help to repair the substandard housing in parts of the city, the children would pay the price. "Studies show that when families live in run-down homes, their kids are more likely to have emotional and educational problems."

"I'll share this in our next session meeting," I assured John. "I'll see what we can do about it."

When the ruling body of the church learned what had happened, they decided the Elkhart congregation needed to get involved. A committee of six was organized, called the Citizens Coalition on Housing and Living Space. They met every Monday evening. Their major concern was finding funds to complete the redevelopment project already under way in the poorest area of Elkhart, known as Benham West.

The committee decided to visit the mayor's office. I had never met the man and wasn't sure what his reaction would be. But I prayed for him and for the success of the meeting. Ten days after contacting his office, we were given an appointment with the mayor, along with the Director of Redevelopment. I had expected the mayor to be dressed in a tailored suit and conservative tie, with neatly combed hair. Instead, he wore blue jeans and a flannel shirt, and his hair was disheveled. He looked as if he had just returned from a construction job.

The mayor was a no-nonsense man of few words. As we put forth our concerns, as concisely as possible, he listened stoically. He then indicated that he was willing to work with us and with the Director of Redevelopment to obtain funds that would continue the project. He formed the Mayor's Housing Council, then turned the chairmanship of it over to me.

We invited various civic organizations that had indicated a concern for low-income housing to join us. Months of committee work followed, in cooperation with representatives from Benham West. But the mayor was slow in following up on his promises of finding funds and external contracts to continue the work.

The council invited the mayor to walk with its members through the neglected neighborhood. I expected him to refuse. But a week after we extended the invitation, the mayor joined us on a tour through a neighborhood in Benham West that needed a helping hand. The press was there with cameras flashing.

One resident, an elderly woman wearing a purple house dress, approached the delegation. The mayor listened quietly as she gave a firsthand account of the residents' plight. She painted a vivid picture of outdated, dangerous electrical systems, rusting or loose pipes, gas leaks, homes infested with rodents, and more.

As press releases spread, others in the community became involved. They sent letters to state and federal officials, requesting reinstatement of the project's finances. In response to those letters, the mayor found funds. And after months of work, the renewal project was completed.

What a powerful witness to the community, as well as for those families who got new homes. This ministry showed that churches and agencies with similar goals could have far more impact as a coalition than by working separately.

Chapter Sixteen

Jo

1

I DISCOVERED QUITE A FEW WOMEN in the Elkhart community who had interests similar to mine. We formed a group called People Who Need People. It was a trans-cultural organization composed of Chinese, African-American, and Caucasian women. Our purpose was to improve human relations across cultures as well as to establish positive relations. We had informative discussions on how different races can work together, understanding Chinese women in American culture and the history of Jewish women in the world.

When the Elkhart community learned about our group, we were invited to speak at churches, civic groups, and schools. We also had many casual social events, including cookouts and dinners where we shared ethnic dishes and recipes. Through dialogue and interactions, we came to understand, appreciate, and accept one another. These relationships greatly enriched our lives.

Every Sunday night I worked at a coffee house where young people in the community gathered to talk and hang out. Most of them were members of motorcycle gangs, with leather jackets, tattoos, and sunglasses. Some were dropouts, on the fringe of society. I wasn't sure if I had enough confidence to relate to these kids, especially after my negative experience with the youth group in Warsaw, but I wanted to give it a try.

To my delight, I found that I could interact quite effectively with these young people. For some reason, they seemed to trust me. One night, one of the toughest teens in Elkhart spent the whole evening talking with me about his life. He was very polite and kind. I gave him a listening ear without judging anything he said. I was hoping it made him feel important.

Another one of the teens asked if he and his fiancée could be married in our church. He was terrified to meet Bill, but he trusted me enough to finally talk with him—and was thrilled when Bill agreed to perform the ceremony.

2

Bill's counseling load became quite heavy. He was always discreet about the people he counseled, never mentioning anyone to me by name. However, one night, as we were getting ready for bed, he teasingly told me that several of the women he was counseling were attracted to him, and some actually flirted with him. He assured me that he did not lead them on.

I knew that my husband's love for me, and his strong moral code, would never let him be unfaithful. So I smiled. "I love that other women find you attractive. That means I have good taste."

He winked at me. "Do you find me attractive?"

I shrugged, then giggled. He wrapped his arms around me and we fell into bed, laughing.

Determined to build up our relationship, we found fun ways of growing our marriage. We went on a date every week, and we got away from the city every so often. We traveled to Chicago to attend the Lyric Opera, to Fort Wayne to eat at an ethnic restaurant, and to Indianapolis to visit friends. These trips allowed us uninterrupted conversation time and reignited the love we had for each other.

Chapter Seventeen

Bill

JANUARY IS A DEPRESSING MONTH for many people. The holidays are over, the weather is bleak, the Christmas-gift bills are due, and it's time to start working on income taxes. Because of these factors and more, there is always an explosion of people needing spiritual counseling during that month. With all my other responsibilities at the Elkhart church, it felt overwhelming at times. But in 1972, I was thrown a lifeline.

I was in my office at the church, working on my sermon, when Dr. Kintner, one of the physicians in the congregation, came to visit me. This middle-aged man walked in with his usual gentle spirit. "Sorry to disturb you, but there's something I'd like to share with you. May I sit down?"

I directed him to a seat in front of my desk.

"I have an idea, but I need your help," he said, and took a deep breath. "Many of my patients have nothing physically wrong with them, but they continue to complain about not feeling well. It's as if something is blocking their wellness. I believe that their problems are rooted in emotions. Stress, grief, anger, depression. They need someone to listen to them, preferably someone with psychological or spiritual counseling skills." He cocked his head. "I'm sure you already have an overload of counseling."

I chuckled. "I certainly do, especially at this time of year." But I couldn't help thinking about the time I had taken off from pastoring to become educated in psychological counseling.

Dr. Kintner asked if there was some way that our two professions could work together. Perhaps provide a place where people could come for medical care and also for counseling. "Doctors could be on staff for the physical exam, and clergy and other professional counselors would be the listening ears."

Excitement bubbled up inside me at the idea. I had read books by Paul Tournier, who was convinced that a person's physical, mental, and spiritual well-being are delicately balanced. I had come to the same conclusion as I counseled with folks in the church. "I think your idea is brilliant!"

"Where could this happen?" Dr. K asked, obviously thrilled with my enthusiasm.

"What about our church building?"

An hour later, my secretary popped her head in the door and said the hospital was calling for Dr. Kintner. Before he left, we made an appointment to discuss the idea further. In the following months, we brainstormed, researched, and talked with other doctors and counselors. Neither Dr. K nor I had time to do the required administrative work. But about that time, Reverend R.J. Ross was hired as the minister of parish life. He was just out of seminary, but he had training in counseling and administration. Dr. K and I knew this man was exactly the right person to help us launch the Samaritan Health and Living Center.

I obtained the consent of the trustees of the church to let the center have rent-free office space. Dr. K found professional support in the medical community—a number of physicians agreed to serve on the board, to refer patients, and to act as consultants. RJ took over the administrative/managerial responsibilities. Clients swarmed in, attracted by the idea of being helped with their medical and psychological issues within the caring atmosphere of the church. The center began on a one-afternoon-a-week basis; within a year it was operating five days a week.

To our amazement, similar centers sprang up all over the country and even in Japan. Dr. K and I were pleased that the idea we had hatched was becoming a worldwide reality.

Today there are more than 470 centers serving 335 communities in the United States and Japan that are accredited and supported by the Samaritan Institute, now headquartered in Denver, Colorado, under the leadership of R.J. Ross.

Chapter Eighteen

Jo

ONE SATURDAY MORNING IN AUGUST, as I was driving the children to K-Mart to buy shoes for school, I heard the screeching of tires against pavement, followed by a loud thud. At the intersection, a young boy, around eleven, lay in the street, his bicycle sprawled near him, wheels still spinning. No other vehicles or people were nearby, except the driver of the truck that had hit the boy. He got out of his vehicle and paced in a daze, seemingly unable to grasp what had just happened.

People started to gather around, but no one tried to help. Against my own fear of seeing a child possibly dying, I jumped out of the car and ran over to the boy. "Call the police," I shouted. "Call an ambulance. Get me a blanket and some towels." Like sleepwalkers being awakened, folks ran to carry out my orders.

The boy called out for his mother and tried to stand. Concerned that any injuries he might have sustained could be intensified by movement, I made sure he stayed as still as possible. Finally, the paramedics arrived. They carefully placed him on a board and transferred him to the ambulance. As they were about to shut the doors, the boy's mother arrived.

"He's going to be okay," I assured her.

"Thank you." She climbed into the ambulance and they headed for the hospital. I returned to our car, and we continued on to K-Mart. All the way there, my children talked about how brave their mother had been.

"Mom," Jeff yelled from the backseat, "you're a hero. You stood out in the crowd!"

I thanked God for His strength, grateful for the outcome and for my children's admiration.

Chapter Nineteen

Bill

Racial tensions ran high in the early 1970s, even in Elkhart, Indiana. Inferior housing, lack of meaningful employment, and limited political representation by minorities often led to violent clashes. Pastors needed to get involved with social issues and with the struggle for civil rights. I wondered how this would affect my wife and my children.

Jo and I were worried that interracial riots, which had become common in many parts of the country, might affect our community. There were rumors that racial clashes could explode at any time, and I knew I had to be at the forefront to help ease tensions. I also needed allies. So, I invited three black friends and two white friends to join me for a brainstorming session at a downtown pub. I knew some of my Christian friends would not approve of the locale. But I hoped it would be a place that would not discriminate, with its festive atmosphere and people from all walks of life.

We arranged to meet on a Friday night, but we told no one else about our plans. My friends and I sat in a corner booth in the back of the restaurant. While the jukebox played Beatles songs, we brainstormed a plan of action. Unlike some of the meetings I had moderated at the church, we all agreed on what could be done to help prevent racial riots in the community. We planned strategies that could be implemented if the need arose.

Halfway through the meeting, Thad, a black member of the group, said, "Bill, I have a friend you've got to meet. His name is Tiny. He weighs two hundred and forty pounds, and he played fullback for Central High. He's one sharp dude, and he knows what's happening in the black community. How about coming with me to see him next week? He runs a bar down in the ghetto. I'll introduce you around."

A week later, Thad escorted me to Tiny's bar. The smell of stale tobacco and beer hung in the air. It took a few seconds for my eyes to adjust to the dimly lit room. A multicolored light hung over the bar. Behind it stood a commanding figure, over six feet tall, with massive hands that seemed to encompass everything they touched. His head was shaved, and his immense arms were covered with colorful tattoos.

After Thad introduced us, Tiny asked me questions, trying to see if I was on the level. Before long the barriers of mistrust fell away. Even though I was the only white person in the place, I felt strangely at home. The apprehensions I felt when I entered the bar vanished quickly. I returned to Tiny's bar several times after that initial visit.

A few months later, as I was preparing to head home from my office, I got a call from Tiny. "We need you down here. There's been some trouble at the high school, and it's getting out of control."

I called Grover, a white member of the group, to start the chain of phone calls. Then I ran to Tiny's bar. When I arrived, panting, Tiny and Jesse hustled me outside.

"We're going to sandwich you between us while we walk the streets together," Jesse said. "Those high schoolers need to see a white man who's a friend to the black man."

Together, we strolled through downtown Elkhart. I stood between Jesse and Tiny, smiling, occasionally speaking a word of greeting to a familiar face. We ended up at the Donut Shop South, where seventy-five black teens were amassed with assorted weapons: two-by-fours, baseball bats, knives, brass knuckles.

We stopped in front of the crowd, and Tiny shook hands with his black brothers, trying to reassure them. Jesse did the same. I just stood there, not sure what I should do.

Tiny turned to me. "Jesse and I are going to Dirker's parking lot to see if Thad and Earl are OK. You stay here for a while and let people know there are some good white folks in the world. In a few minutes, come on over and join us." They took off toward the viaduct, leaving me standing there alone, a white island in a sea of scared, angry black faces. I was terrified, but I stood there smiling, hoping they would see I was a friend.

I found out later what happened on the other side of that viaduct.

Tiny and Jesse came upon a swarm of white people, marching four abreast, carrying lead pipes, wrenches, broken glass, and other weapons. Chanting the popular derogatory term of the time for African Americans, the group headed for the entrance to the underpass, where their black "enemies" were encamped.

As the marchers neared the parking lot of Dirker's department store, four police cars pulled into the street and blocked both entrances to the viaduct. Thad and Earl emerged from two police cars with two white policemen. The drivers of the other two police cars were black. Their white passengers stepped into the street.

The angry marchers gathered in the parking lot. Their leader shouted orders. Thad and Earl jumped up on the loading dock. His black face shining with perspiration, Earl bellowed, "I'm a nigger."

Everyone turned, in shock at what they had heard.

"I have been all my life."

"Shut your face," someone yelled.

A few people in the crowd threw sticks and trash at Earl. One of the sticks hit his kneecap. He flinched in pain, but he went on. "I hear one of your buddies got beat up by a black man. I don't blame you for being mad. That'd make me angry enough to spit in the face of the guy who done it. I'd want to blacken both of his eyes."

His words enraged the crowd. Some shouted obscenities. Others stomped on tin cans to drown out the sound of his words.

On the other side of the underpass, I was coping with my own chaos. Not long after Tiny and Jesse left, I felt a growing restlessness among the seventy-five blacks whose turf I was sharing. I tried to lighten the mood by joking with a few, but that didn't work. I saw fear and anger in the faces of my black brothers. Not knowing what else to do, I stood there and watched and listened. As the crowd became more agitated, a thin young man slithered over to where I stood. "If I was you, I'd be on my way. You done served your purpose here."

At that moment, two white motorcyclists revved their engines and began circling the spot where I stood. They drew closer and closer, headlights blazing in the disappearing daylight, until they were within inches of my knees.

I managed to slip between the two cyclists and head for the underpass in search of Tiny and Jesse. I found my friends at the edge of more than a hundred whites, watching Earl and Thad on the platform. Without hesitation they placed me between them.

One of the rednecks hollered, "Ain't they cute! Look at that Oreo cookie with the turncoat white center."

I shifted my weight and took deep breaths, trying to fight off the dizziness that suddenly engulfed me. Tiny stood next to me, fists clenched as others picked up the chant: "Ain't they cute! Ain't they cute!"

More police arrived and fanned out around the crowd. But the whites didn't move. Tiny, Jesse, and I waited on the outskirts of the crowd while Thad kept talking, painting a picture of what it was like to be a black man in a white man's world.

Suddenly, Thad stopped talking, and he and Earl jumped down from the platform. They wove through the crowd, shaking hands with a few of the whites. This simple act, and the presence of the police, helped calm the crowd. Slowly, they dispersed.

On the other side of the viaduct, the blacks waited, prepared for a confrontation. Thad and Earl, accompanied by the police, headed for the Donut Shop South. Tiny, Jesse, and I followed. Tiny faced the edgy crowd and waved them to be quiet. He explained what had happened. I felt their palpable relief upon finding out that the whites had gone home and the threat of danger was over. The crowd broke apart and scattered in all directions.

I finally breathed.

Chapter Twenty

Jo

AFTER THE INCIDENT AT DIRKER'S DEPARTMENT STORE, our life returned to normal. Other than some undercurrents of unrest, the neighborhoods seemed tranquil. And the Vamos family was happy, busy, and thriving.

Becky, a senior in high school, had many achievements to be proud of. She was a class officer, member of the National Honor Society, and candidate for the Miss USA pageant. She had lots of friends. She took voice lessons, mainly to please me, which helped her land a lead role as the duchess in her school's production of *The Sound of Music*.

Susan, age nine, also auditioned for the musical and was awarded the part of the talkative Brigitte—a perfect fit for her. At home she was our bright star, always full of joy and laughter. Her report cards were good, and she presented her oral assignments in creative, often dramatic ways.

Jeff, at sixteen, was growing up to be a well-rounded young man. His ears had disappeared behind thick brown hair, he no longer needed glasses, and his athletic body undoubtedly made him attractive to many of the high school girls. Jeff had several interests. Cross-country and track took up much of his time. He enjoyed writing and became editor of the school newspaper. But his principal hobby was furniture making, a skill he learned at school and supplemented by doing his own research.

Bill, in spite of his busy schedule and all the challenges of his life, always made time for the children. He loved coming home to a house bursting with happy sounds: me singing, Becky playing the piano, Jeff on the violin, and Susan dancing around the house on her tiptoes.

Bill seldom missed any of the kids' school activities. When the girls were in *The Sound of Music*, we both attended all four performances, and at every one, tears of pride flowed down Bill's cheeks. He watched all of Jeff's track and cross-country meets, regardless of how far away they were held, and his shouts of encouragement to his son could probably be heard three counties away.

For me, life felt joyful and balanced. I received appreciation for my singing, I was working with the senior high students at church again, and the group was growing and flourishing. I felt proud to be Bill's wife. We had a lively social life with lots of interesting friends.

But like rain clouds breaking through on a sunny day, the thunder storms of life soon threatened again.

When the community choir director asked me to sing the role of the good mother in Handel's *Solomon*, I felt like a kid who'd been handed an ice cream cone for the first time. The group included music majors from Indiana University—heady company to be among. So as not to look foolish, I worked hard on the part. But all my insecurities from the harsh years in Warsaw returned with a vengeance. I leaned heavily on Bill for support and affirmation.

Though Bill had his own problems, including budgetary concerns and the need to dismiss a staff member, he did his best to encourage and reassure me. But his words weren't enough to calm my anxieties about being an amateur among professionals—and with a leading role, no less.

On the night of the performance, I swept aside my lingering doubts and focused on enjoying the fruits of all my hard work. As I stepped onto the stage in that large auditorium, I sneaked a peek at

Bill in the second row. He smiled up at me. I was at peace, knowing he was praying for me.

Free from the fear of failure, I sang the role with compassion and confidence, just like the good mother in Solomon must have felt for her son. At the end of my solo, I sat down and looked into the audience again. Tears were falling down Bill's cheeks.

After the performance, there was a short celebration for the cast. But seeing the exhaustion in Bill's eyes, I skipped the party. The stress of the preceding few weeks had clearly begun to catch up with him.

I shouldn't have leaned so heavily on him. He managed to hide his inner turmoil from everyone else, but I sensed it.

Chapter Twenty-One

Bill

A FULL YEAR AFTER THE INCIDENT at Dirker's department store, I was still constantly attacked by an unmanageable inner turbulence. I couldn't stop worrying. I couldn't sleep, even with an increased dose of sleeping pills.

I went for counseling, but that didn't stop the incessant tension that was convulsing me. Seeing no other option, I told the church board that I needed a leave of absence. Then I went home, picked up Jo, and drove to the hospital in Fort Wayne, Indiana, an hour and a half away. Physically, I felt as if someone were scraping a wire brush inside my stomach and chest.

Soon after we arrived, I was admitted to the psych ward. Jo knew there was nothing she could do so she left for home.

Even after I was taken to a private room, my mind kept pinching me with relentless staccato thoughts.

Think I'll go to my room and relax now.

No, can't do that. My sermon for Sunday isn't done yet.

This world is coming to an end.

Do they all know how scared I am?

Jesus is coming, and He might be me.

I don't recognize anyone here, but their faces are all ugly.

I tried to concentrate on just one thought. Any thought. But I couldn't.

A nurse took me to the hospital dining room. It was empty. I sat at a table while the nurse went to the cafeteria line and got me a tray of food. I stared at the dishes she put in front of me, paralyzed yet about to explode.

I have to hold on. I clutched the edges of the table until my knuckles turned white. Suddenly, everything inside me was swept into a raging sea of adrenalin, as though every nerve in my body were blowing up at the same time. I jumped from my chair and ran for the nurse's station, where I lunged at the thick window that protected the ladies in white uniforms. As I reached up to strike the window, two muscular hands grabbed my wrist from behind and halted my heaving body.

"Hey, buddy, take it easy." The voice was as friendly as the hands were strong.

I swung around and saw a large man with a shaved head, tattoos, and kindness in his eyes. He let go of me, smiled, and extended his hand. "Hi, Bill. My name's Fred. I'm one of the orderlies here." There was no irritation in his voice, only genuine sympathy. "How about you come with me. There's a special place here we call the Frustration Room. You can do anything you want there: scream, beat on the walls, cry, sing, sleep—even laugh. C'mon."

The rushing adrenalin in my body felt like a flood of brown-and-gray panic. Fred took me to a room that looked like a white cave and handed me two padded sticks. "Here, cut loose with these." After telling me he would be back, he locked the door behind him.

The ceiling seemed to descend on my head. I tried to find an opening in the four walls. With a frenzy I flailed the padded sticks, first on one wall, then another, and another. I beat the walls as I ran in circles. I finally stopped, and with all my strength, I tried to break down the wall in front of me. I hit it so many times that I broke the rubber grip on the stick. Padding spewed over the floor like popcorn. I picked up the sponge pieces and hurled them at the walls and ceiling. Then I picked up the other padded stick and started hitting the walls again. Soon most of the floor was sprinkled with spongy stuff.

I finally sat down, my heart thumping so fast I couldn't hear anything else. My clothes were soaked with sweat. But my eyes were dry, for there were no tears left in me. During gasps for breath, my brain clicked into its familiar rhythm of ceaseless, scary thoughts.

You know that it's happened, don't you?

I can hardly breathe.

The world is coming to an end.

Jesus is coming, and He could be me.

I'm a prisoner.

Roses smell so good. But this floor stinks.

I've got to escape.

I looked at the wall across from me and realized there was a window in my jail cell. I felt as if I'd found buried treasure. Thin metal rods stretched across the glass like a large version of tic-tac-toe. I ran to the window. I clawed the bars with my fingers and beat my hands against them until my fingers turned black and blue.

You know that it's happened, don't you? The voice in my head repeated its sinister threats. *You're leaving the human race for good now. Do those roses smell good? I can't believe how much that floor stinks.*

I fell to the floor and tried to calm down, but the inferno within had burned away every particle of peace I had ever known. I only sat for a second or two before jumping back up. My brain and my body were under the control of perpetual movement. I ran around the room, faster and faster. Finally, I stopped and leaned forward against one wall. My hand fell against a metal object attached to the wall. It was smooth, round, and heavy. I circled both hands around it and gripped it so tightly that only pain forced me to let go. In a moment of clarity, I realized that I had run blindly into the door and was now trying to break off the door knob.

A voice spoke softly from the other side of the door. "You can come out when you've settled down."

The words had no meaning. My incomprehensible thoughts continued to race.

You're no gardener, your feet are too heavy.

Where's the stinking orange juice?

166

Gotta open this jail cell.

The world is coming to an end.

Jesus is coming, and He might be me.

Gotta escape.

I let go of the knob and kicked the door as hard as I could. It didn't budge. I kicked it again, this time shouting and screaming while I attacked. I stopped for a second, panting like a rabid dog, and listened for some sound on the other side. Nothing came. So I kicked and shouted and screamed again. And again. And again.

Those stinking, rotten roses are spoiling the orange juice.

With each assault on the door, I lost more consciousness of who I was. Was I even still human? I felt nothing. No feelings, no jumping nerve ends or adrenalin, not even any pain or confusion. I ran around the room again, this time using my arms and legs as if I were a monkey. I crawled across the floor, lay on my back, and bellowed. I scraped the floor for food. I had no control of myself. Nothing functioned except for my memory, clearly recording it all so I could see it vividly, for the rest of my life, as though it were happening all over again.

Somewhere, in the choking grip of psychosis, I fell asleep.

Chapter Twenty-Two

Jo

I LEFT THE PSYCH WARD of the Fort Wayne Hospital in a daze. *Why is this happening again?* Defeat crushed my spirit.

I headed to my car. The shadows peeking through the cement openings of the parking garage cast ominous figures on the walls and floor. I walked up to the spot where I'd parked our car, but it wasn't there. I searched from one floor to the next, panicked and exhausted. *Concentrate, Jo. Where did you leave it?* I had no idea.

Suddenly the dam broke. Bracing myself against a cement pillar, I wept uncontrollably.

Oh, why, why, why did Bill have to get sick again? Our family was happy in Elkhart. The doctors are not even sure what's wrong with him.

After several moments of paralyzing agony, I pulled myself together and resumed the search for my sedan. I was shaking by the time I finally found it, hiding behind a large white pickup. I sank into the driver's seat.

As I drove back to Elkhart, Christmas lights dotted the landscape. But my mind couldn't think about the holiday just two weeks away. The house was quiet when I stumbled though the back door. Mother and the children were asleep. In the kitchen, I noticed the flowers on the table had dried before they were able to bloom. That was exactly how I felt.

I shuffled to our bedroom. Life felt empty, hopeless. I kicked off my shoes and fell into bed, praying for sleep, wishing I could block out all my thoughts and feelings. But they kept coming, slamming into one another. Life had never hurt so much.

A sudden chill in the room made me reach for the blanket at the foot of the bed. Outside, snow had accumulated on the window sill. It looked like white cotton candy. Snow-laden trees glistened under the street lights, making the night beautiful. But my world had lost its sparkle.

I need You, God. I am angry, even with You. But I will still trust You.

Chapter Twenty-Three

Bill

1

I AWOKE, FEELING NUMB, lying on my stomach with my head nestled in my arms.

While I slept, someone had brought a mattress into the Frustration Room and placed it just below the window. Darkness sifted its way into every corner of the room, except for a shaft of welcoming light beckoning to me through the thick, dirty window pane. For a while I floated in the untroubled waters of no feelings at all. It was almost peaceful.

The light outside kept inviting me to bathe in its brightness. I slowly lifted my body and looked out at the street. My eyes squinted at the blazing rays of a street light. It revealed a cracked sidewalk and an old, white frame house with black shutters. The front porch had red brick steps. There was something special about that house. I felt as if, somehow, God was using it to assure me that He was thinking of me.

I heard somebody praying. A familiar male voice pleaded, "Oh, God, let Bill know that You love him even now. Lift him up with Your arms." I recognized the voice of my brother-in-law, Dave Neely. For Dave, prayer was like food. But he prayed to feed the inner person.

Dave lived about five hundred miles away, yet I could hear his prayer whispering within me. "Lift Bill up, Lord. Lift him up with Your arms." As I watched the friendly house across the street, I listened to Dave's voice. Sleep finally came again—this time on the mattress rather than on the hard floor.

I woke up with a jolt, as if an electric wire had shocked my brain. I jerked to a sitting position and snapped to attention. I smelled something foul. *Where am I?*

The voices returned.

It's the end of the world.

Jesus is coming, and He could be me.

Like a frothing animal, I roved the room, searching for food, growling, whining, crying, screaming. In the midst of my whirling and raving, I hit my head on the floor and passed out.

When I regained consciousness, I was in a bed, my hands and feet held fast to the bed frame by thick leather shackles. My mind broiled with anger.

Think they can make a prisoner of me, do they?

The shackles were just loose enough to allow my arms and legs to move slightly. Using my torso as a pump, and my legs and arms as handles, I propelled myself and the heavy metal bed around the room, yelling, "Here I come. You'd better be ready!"

I hauled myself and the bed to a spot just in front of the door. Heaving, I slammed the bed against the heavy wood, over and over and over. Finally, my energy drained. Slippery from sweat, I collapsed.

Gosh, those roses stink.

Stop smelling. Sleep is coming, one wave at a time.

God, lift me up with Your loving arms.

The cool waters of slumber covered my body and gave me the precious miracle of rest.

2

When I awoke again, the morning sun shone through the window, warming my body. I was lying on a mattress on the floor. The shackles were gone, and the door was open. For the first time in what could have been days or weeks or months, my head felt as though it was attached to my body. My eyes burned, my hair itched, and my breath smelled like spoiled bananas. My hands were swollen and puffy, like black-and-blue work gloves. My wrists were red and raw, with deep scratches. So were my ankles. Every particle of my body was sore.

Hot, salty tears slid down my cheeks. I shuddered from a halting deep breath that shook my aching shoulders. I hurt everywhere—and it was a soothing, magnificent relief. I could feel my body! I was going to be human again. Yes, there was a winding, jagged, up-and-down road ahead. But I knew I would make the journey. I would live again.

"Why?" I asked.

The answer tumbled right into my question. *God lifted you up, Bill. He held on. He never once let go.*

Fred stepped into the Frustration Room, carrying a breakfast tray. "You must be awful hungry. This is your first meal in four days." He set the tray on the floor beside me. Bacon and eggs, with toast and coffee, beckoned me. I sat up, letting the intoxicating smells penetrate a brain that had forgotten how to process sensory stimuli.

"You sure had us all worried, Bill. You crashed so bad; everything broke apart at once. But you look different this morning. Peaceful, calm." Fred encircled me in a welcoming embrace, as if the arms of God were holding me. Then he sat on the floor beside me while I ate.

Eating breakfast was a slow and struggling ordeal. The process of chewing and swallowing was awkward and sometimes painful, but, one careful bite at a time, I ate every morsel. I felt the contentment of a full stomach for the first time in four days.

With renewed physical strength and courage, I said, "I need to know what happened to me in here, Fred. I mean, I feel like the most sick, miserable, out of control, ugly human being on earth. What's wrong with me?"

Fred hesitated for a moment, then responded: "You went through drug withdrawal, Bill."

"No, no, I'm no addict," I protested, "I preach against drug addiction and I hold drug programs for our youth. You're way off base."

Fred looked down at the floor and then he turned his face toward me. "Bill, how many years were you on sleeping pills?"

I gasped. *Sleeping pills!* It felt as if someone had punched me.

He repeated the question: "Bill, how many years were you on sleeping pills?"

I searched my mind for the answer. Then it all came spilling out: "I was twenty-one when I started and I'm forty-three now; twenty-two years. My doctor said they were strong but couldn't hurt me. He said some people take them for fifty years. I told him I was taking them every night, and he said that was no problem."

"What kind of sleeping pills?" Fred's question pressured me, but his eyes kept telling me he only wanted to listen, so I named the sleeping pills I had used through the years.

Fred took a deep breath. "Those are some of the most powerful sleep medications you could possibly take." He laid his hand gently on my shoulder. "Your doctor led you into drug addiction. You were choking yourself inside your body. For the last four days your body has been screaming for help."

"All the hell I've been through since I've been in this place has happened because I have a chemical dependency?"

"Well, I can't say that." Fred shrugged. "You'll have to talk to your doctor to get the full story. I'm just telling you that you were on one great big withdrawal trip. And here's the important thing: It's over, and it doesn't ever have to happen again."

I couldn't stop the tears from falling as I released the pain and worry that had held me so tightly for such a long time. Beside me,

I could hear Fred's gentle voice. "Don't be ashamed of those tears, man. It's a sign that healing is coming."

I wanted to tell Fred that he must be one of God's angels. But the words wouldn't come out.

"You want to rest awhile?" he asked. "Or would you prefer to do some more talking?"

I stretched out on the mattress, eased my head onto the pillow, and tried closing my eyes. They insisted on staying open, so I started talking. Once I began, I couldn't stop.

"It all began my senior year in college when I was twenty-one. A deliciously beautiful girl was wearing my fraternity pin. I was a leader on campus. I had a good part-time job. I was studying hard. Then it happened: like an avalanche of liquid panic, anxiety poured through my body. There was no waiting for a wayward loved one, no crisis, no cause at all, except some nameless, threatening enemy inside me.

"Once in a while I got a little relief, for a day or two. In fact, there was a period for about four weeks when I felt absolutely great, almost unconquerable. This was strange, because, just as soon as I was sure I had it made, the volcano inside me erupted again, and anxiety reigned once more, as the ruler of my life."

A tear rolled down Fred's cheek. "You have been through so much, Bill. But God is with you. You know that, don't you?" Fred stopped, embarrassed by his own childlike tenderness. He kept listening with his heart as I continued to share my fears of going back to my parish after a "leave of absence" in a psych ward. And writing sermons again, with no power to concentrate. And whether my family would accept me back. And how long I would look like a very sick person.

Fred listened closely, his eyes reflecting concern for me. Talking was like cleaning out my insides; it was also exhausting. My breathing and speech became slower. I yawned, and my eyelids fluttered. Like a curtain at the finale of a long and tragic drama, they closed.

Eleven hours later, I was startled by a sharp rapping on the door.

"Hey, is anybody in there? This is Theodore. It's orange juice time."

I tried to focus. Where was I? The words "orange juice" roused my taste buds. Then I remembered Theodore. Every night, he served orange juice to the residents of Psych Ward 86.

"Come in," I mumbled, struggling to open my eyes.

Theodore burst through the door like a breathless messenger about to announce unbelievably good news. As I drank my juice, he told me part of his story. He had lived in Psych Ward 86 for ten years. He was no longer "sick," but he had no place to go, so he stayed here.

"When the doctor first told me I had to stick around, I hated the idea of rotting away with all these loonies. But I found out the folks in here aren't loonies at all. They're people, with special problems. I saw them taking care of each other. They're not afraid to admit they're needy, and they're not afraid to help. In here, nobody thinks he's better than anybody else. We're all in the same boat. So we row together."

I liked the sound of that. "Do you ever leave here?"

"Every week I get an eight-hour pass. I go to the park and feed the chipmunks and the crows. But you know what? When I'm out there, I miss everyone in here. These people are my family. And I get two or three new brothers and sisters every few weeks. The tough part is saying good-bye to those who leave. Want some more OJ?"

Theodore filled my glass, then headed for the door. "You're going to be OK, kid. You've got a tiny glimmer in your eyes. It's going to get brighter." Theodore hustled down the hall, looking for his next brother or sister to serve.

I spent some part of the day in group therapy and the remainder of the day resting. That night I slept peacefully. At seven the next morning, Fred brought me more juice . . . and some exciting news.

"Doc says you can move back to the room where you stayed your first night in the hospital."

Fred helped me pick up my few belongings and escorted me to my old room. It was bleak, but it had two windows, three roommates, and a dresser drawer for my underwear and toiletries. It took lots of concentration to decide where to put things in that drawer.

For the next several days, I went to the cafeteria and group therapy with plodding uncertainty. But the intense, uncontrollable anxiety was beginning to leave me. I felt insecure yet peaceful. A calm started to grow within me.

I wondered how Jo was doing. I'd been told she came to visit often, but I was too sick to know she was there. Now I longed to see her.

My roommates tried to get me to exercise with them, but my body was too weak from the private war I had fought in the Frustration Room. That was OK with me; what I needed was time alone. A quiet place where I could read and pray.

My previous prayers had all been pleas for emergency help, like calling for a spiritual ambulance. I still prayed those prayers, but I also added a few prayers for the people in Psych Ward 86. I even said "thank you" to God a time or two, although I limited my gratitude for fear that too many thanksgivings might stop the blessings of feeling better, as though God was going to say, "Well, he's thankful now. That's enough help for him."

Only three days after I settled into my new surroundings, Fred announced that I would be moving to an apartment. Excitement filled my mind. Followed almost immediately by doubts. *I'm being released already? It's too soon, isn't it?*

But I was doing better. My thinking was much clearer. I felt stronger. That emotional teeter-totter still pushed my insides up and down, but it wasn't so terrible anymore. I was panicking a little less and enjoying being myself a little more.

I wondered what the apartment would be like. As I was about to ask Fred, he said, "You'd better start packing. You've got to be out of here as soon as possible."

We quickly packed up my few possessions, including several get-well cards from my wife and various church members, and headed for the apartment. We didn't have to walk far because it was part of the hospital.

My "apartment" was a large room with a private bathroom. It had a dresser, two stuffed chairs, and a larger bed than in my hospital room. There were no bars on the window, just faded brown curtains.

I unpacked my belongings and arranged my greeting cards on the dresser top. As I stepped back to admire my new surroundings, Dr. Grayling, my new doctor from Fort Wayne, appeared in the doorway. With a smile, he sat in one of the chairs, motioning me to take the other. We looked at each other in silence for a moment.

"Two things," he said with his usual crisp precision. "One, you're going home in five days. That'll be Christmas Eve."

I held my breath for fear he would take back those words.

"Two, we've diagnosed the problem."

My heart raced. If the cause of my problems had been determined, a cure must be possible.

He continued, "I was puzzled when I tried various medications and approaches for schizophrenia and none of them seemed to help. Then something in your medical history caught my attention, and I realized that you'd been misdiagnosed. You're not schizophrenic, like your original doctor thought. Your disease is manic depression, otherwise known as bipolar disorder."

Tears flowed—tears of anger and relief. Finally, someone had found the cause of my inner turmoil. But what did the diagnosis mean?

"Manic depression is caused by a genetic chemical imbalance," Dr. Grayling explained. "There's a mineral that can keep your body chemistry balanced. It's not a drug or a tranquilizer, just an ordinary mineral that's mined in the earth. It's called lithium. You've been taking it for five days. This mineral will keep things in balance—not so many pushes and shoves, ups and downs. Essentially, you'll be a new man. All you have to do is take your lithium at the prescribed times, develop healthy eating and sleeping habits, and exercise whenever you can. Do that and you've got a new life ahead."

"That's it?"

"That's it!" Dr. Grayling slapped his hands on his knees, stood, shook hands with me, and walked out the door.

I sat there motionless, trying to process what I had just heard. Could the doctor be right? Was it possible for me to live a normal, healthy life?

I thought about seeing my family on Christmas: snow, church, music, grandparents, coffee cake, presents, stockings full of toys, and the celebration of the birth of the Christ Child.

I remembered the first Christmas Jo and I spent together after we were married, when we had no money and decided one gift was all we could afford. Indiana's cold, snowy winters persuaded us that the best thing we could give ourselves was a snow shovel.

I recalled the birth of our beautiful daughter on Christmas Day. Even though I'd resented her intrusion into my marriage before she was born, the minute she was placed in my arms, I adored her.

I couldn't remember a bad Christmas.

I was basking in happy memories when a rap on the door interrupted my thoughts. A familiar face peeked in the door. It was Dorothy Ransom, the woman on the pulpit committee who had left such a good impression on Jo, and who was now was a close family friend as well as a hard-working member of the church. "Could you stand to see a friend who misses you?"

"Of course, Dorothy, come in."

She scurried toward my chair.

I stood to greet her with a hug. "Thanks for coming. I'm really glad you're here, because I just received some good news from the doctor. He's releasing me. I get to go home in five days, and he claims that I will be well."

She sat down in one of the chairs, beaming at me. "I knew you could do it. Some folks in the church were concerned, even scared.

But I knew God would come through. Oh, Bill, the congregation will be thrilled that you're coming home."

I took a deep breath and sat beside her. "Do you really think they all want me to come back? Or are there some who think I've let them down? After all, I've been in a psych ward. And I don't look very healthy."

"Some of them may doubt you, Bill," she said softly. "But you have no idea how much the people of the church respect and trust you."

"To be honest, I'm kind of scared to go back to the church. I'll have to win everyone's confidence all over again."

She nodded slowly. "Yes, a few of them will test you. Some people are never satisfied. But that was true before you left."

I chuckled. She was right about that.

"Most of us want you back as soon as possible. We miss our pastor and your preaching. We know you will keep on caring for us, and we want to support you."

"Do you really think so?" I wanted to believe what she said. But my stubborn fears lingered.

Dorothy cocked her head and looked me in the eye. "Have I ever been dishonest with you?"

"Of course not!"

At that moment, Jo walked in, carrying a box of chocolates and a copy of the daily newspaper. "I hope I'm not interrupting." She smiled at Dorothy.

"Absolutely not, but I've got to get going." Dorothy rose, gave us each a hug, and left.

My heart leaped at seeing my wife. But Jo stood at a distance, and an awkward silence fell between us, as if we were separated by an invisible divider. Was she still seeing me as a mental-hospital patient? I could almost hear her thoughts. *Can I trust this fragile person standing before me? Is he really well?*

In an obvious effort to break the tension, Jo walked around the room, wearing a painted smile as she pointed out insignificant little details, like the dingy curtains. "What a comfortable, cozy room."

I stood up, and we embraced. It had been so long since I held her, I wanted it to last forever. Finally, she pulled back a bit, looked into my eyes, and caressed my stubbled cheek. "You still look a little peaked, but much better."

"I feel a lot better. But what about you? How are you holding up?"

"Oh, I'm fine." She focused on the dresser, her face stoic.

"Be honest. How do you really feel?"

She sighed. "I admit, it's been pretty rough. Most of the time, I'm torn between my faith and my anger. I shout at God sometimes. But I know He's giving me the strength to continue."

I could relate.

"Oh, Bill!" She reached for me and I held her. "I just hope there's some good reason for all this pain." She convulsed into weeping.

"There will be." I drew her closer. "Everything's going to be OK."

I held her for a long time, letting her sob on my shoulder. When she lifted her head, she wiped away her tears and put on a sunny face. "One good thing has already come out of this is. The children have gotten to know their grandmother better. Mom has been an anchor in this storm. And she's been praying for you every day."

"Please thank her for me."

We settled on the small sofa, and I took her hand. "Hey, I have some good news. I'll be home on Christmas Eve."

"Really?" Jo jumped into my lap and kissed my face repeatedly.

I laughed. "Wait, there's more. Doc Grayling knows what's been wrong with me and he's going to help."

As I told her the details, we hugged and cried and laughed.

"I have exciting news too," Jo said with a grin.

"What is it?"

Jo hopped off of my lap and clasped her hands together. "The church officers have voted to give you a six-month sabbatical to rest, read, and write. They've even arranged for our family to stay in a little home on Sanibel Island, Florida, for the whole six months." She grabbed my hands and pulled me to my feet. We clapped and cheered and danced around the room until I was so tired I had to lie down. Realizing I needed my rest, Jo planted a kiss on my forehead and slipped quietly out of the room.

I drifted off to sleep with happy thoughts. In my mind, I kept repeating, "I'll be home on Christmas Eve. I'm getting a sabbatical. And I'm going to be healthy." I needed time for the news to sink in. I felt like a man sitting at a banquet table, a delicious meal before him, unable to open his mouth.

Chapter Twenty-Four

Jo

1

I PICKED BILL UP from the Fort Wayne hospital mid-afternoon on Christmas Eve. As we drove back to Elkhart, my husband looked tired. "How's the family doing?" he asked.

"You'd be so proud of the kids. They've all pitched in to help Mother, doing whatever she needs. Jeffrey was determined we wouldn't go without a Christmas tree, so he took it upon himself to find one. He put it in the stand all by himself, and he and the girls decorated it. It looks beautiful."

I talked about what a gift my mother's presence had been. "I can't believe this is the first Christmas she's spent with us since we got married."

Bill shrugged. "She said she felt more comfortable spending the holidays with sister Miriam and her family. Probably because we've always been so busy with church responsibilities at Christmas."

When I glanced at Bill, I saw a tear creep down his pale face. I drove the rest of the way in silence. But my mind whirled with concerned thoughts.

This was the first time the children had been made aware of Bill's illness. In all the earlier hospitalizations, they were either too young or had not been born yet. The only father they knew was the one they adored and admired. For Becky, he was a listening ear. For Jeff, someone he could count on. And Susan loved the bedtime stories he made up for her. They would be so excited when he got home. We looked forward to our lives as we had known them before this hospitalization.

2

"We're home," I yelled as Bill and I walked into the house. The sweet smell of prune bread filled the air. The children came running, threw their arms around their father, and gave him hugs of love.

"We're so glad you're back," Jeff said. The girls jumped up and down, grateful to have their father back home.

Mother lingered in the kitchen, making split-pea soup, allowing the children to have some time with their father. When Bill managed to break loose, he went to the kitchen, with the children right behind him, and gave my mother a gentle hug. "It's about time you get here," she said with a wink. Then, with a look of compassion, she said, "We're glad you're home."

"Thanks. I'm glad too."

Bill's eyes drooped, and I heard fatigue in his voice. When I suggested that he might want to rest before supper, he said, "Maybe just a short nap," and slipped into the bedroom.

An hour later he emerged, just as we were serving the soup and rolls Mother had prepared. After polishing off the simple but nutritious meal, we all enjoyed prune bread for dessert. Then eighteen-year-old Becky took her father's hand and led him to the living room, with Jeff and Susan not far behind. Deciding the dishes could wait, Mother and I hurried to join them.

Signs of Christmas were everywhere. The white lights on the tree twinkled on and off, reflecting on the angel figurines, snuggled in greenery, lining the mantle. Becky settled her father into his favorite oversized chair in front of the fireplace. She then seated

Mother, Jeff, and me on the orange sofa across the room, facing Bill. Susan sat at her father's feet, her head leaning against his leg.

Later, while the adults sat in front of a crackling fire, the children surprised us with a Christmas program that Becky had written and directed, hoping it would bring a smile to their father's face. She began by reading the Christmas story from the gospel of Luke. When she finished, Jeff picked up his violin and played a piece he had played in church the Sunday before. Susan followed with a reading of "The Night before Christmas." Then Becky played several pieces on the piano, ending with "O Holy Night." As we listened with joy to the gifts our children so generously gave us, tears streamed down our faces.

If strangers had looked through the window that Christmas Eve, they would have assumed that this was the perfect family, not realizing the extent of our deep suffering. But while I had been prepared for a sad Christmas, the children made it a joyful celebration. Though there were few packages under the tree, the gifts of love we received from one another were priceless. God had blessed us with the promise of new hope and new life.

3

If there is such a thing as a perfect place for a six-month family sabbatical, Sanibel Island in Florida would be it.

The church had rented a little house for us near the J. N. Ding Darling National Wildlife Refuge, where alligators occasionally passed by our home in the middle of the night. All was quiet around us, except for the gentle wind and the birds singing love songs throughout the day.

Soon after we arrived, we enrolled the children in school. A bus picked up Becky and Jeff and took them to Fort Myers High. Susan attended the little grade school a few miles away. Driving Susan to school was the only "job" I had during those six months.

The rest of the day, I enjoyed life, doing things I never had time for at home in Indiana.

Bill and I made friends with the pastor of the little island church we attended. We confided in Steve and Carol Evans about Bill's illness, and they played an important part in our emotional healing. It felt good to finally be open about the disease and how it had affected our lives.

Like a mother hen, Carol took me under her wing. She introduced me to shelling and jewelry making and other crafts made from shells. Sanibel is known for the abundance of beautiful seashells found in the Gulf of Mexico. I wandered along the beaches early in the morning, just as the sun lifted its head above the horizon, covering the sand with brilliant light. All the accumulated sadness of the past seemed to fade away as I followed the trail of gifts from the sea.

When Carol learned I could sing, she insisted that I share my gift at several of the worship services. This also became part of my healing.

I was grateful when Steve invited Bill to preach in his pulpit on several Sundays. He was aware that preaching would not be easy after such a long absence. He felt that would help to restore Bill's confidence. And he was right.

Bill spent much of his time writing a book, titled *The Life that Listens*. The publishing company chose that title, and I believe it captured the essence of this man who truly listens with his heart.

Although each of us was involved with our own activities, this six-month sabbatical was a special time for the family. There were no night meetings or any other pastoral duties for Bill. I spent more time cooking, and the children enjoyed playing family games at night, with weekend picnics on the beach.

I wanted to anchor ourselves in this ideal place forever. But the six months passed quickly, and on a humid day in June we loaded up the car with boxes of shells, driftwood, and other treasures we'd found and headed back to Indiana.

4

The thought of returning to the church was scary for Bill. He kept wondering if the congregation really wanted him back. The church was aware that he'd had a breakdown. We could no longer hide behind excuses like vacations or exhaustion. I wasn't sure what the reaction of the church members would be, either, but there had been an outpouring of caring: flowers, food, phone calls, notes of concern. Our family had been surrounded in a circle of love.

When we got back to our familiar Cape Cod home, we got our answer. Every room was vacuumed and dusted, and in the refrigerator we found an entire meal that had been prepared for us. The church women had been busy! Phone calls of welcome poured in. "We're so glad you're home." "We missed you." Without question, our church family was happy to have us back.

On the first Saturday evening following our sabbatical, the working body of the church held a welcome-home reception for our family. We shook hands for a long time as folks patiently waited in line to greet us. I was concerned about Bill standing for so long, but he seemed invigorated by the outpouring of love.

He returned to his work with renewed strength, relaxed, free from the anxiety that had plagued him most of his adult life. The lithium helped to balance his body chemistry, much like a diabetic who takes insulin. The medication made him feel more relaxed. It became as much a part of his life as eating and sleeping.

5

We'd been back in Elkhart exactly a year when we received a phone call from the hospital in Cincinnati, informing us that Bill's father had died. We were saddened by the news, especially since we'd just started getting to know him and developing a relationship with him. He had been a silent presence in our lives—sitting in his recliner, hiding behind the newspaper, puffing away on his pipe—until Bill's mother died eight years before. After that, he learned to interact with the family. He showed interest in what the children were doing, taught them silly songs, and helped them with their homework whenever he visited. We'd invited him to join us on some vacation trips, which he thoroughly enjoyed.

About six months before his death, we were sitting around the kitchen table, eating his favorite meal of chicken and noodles with chocolate pie for dessert. He chatted happily about his life as a corporate executive. Then he turned to Bill and said, "I envy your profession, Bill. I may make money, but you really help people."

Bill beamed. It was just what he'd always needed from his father: confirmation that he was proud of him. I gave Bill's hand a squeeze, knowing how much those words of affirmation meant to him.

Chapter Twenty-Five

Bill

1

ON THE WAY HOME FROM MY FATHER'S FUNERAL, the car suddenly stopped. I managed to coast to the side of the highway and looked under the hood, but couldn't locate the cause of the problem. Jo and Becky walked to a house three hundred yards up the road, but found no one at home. Susan and I stayed with the car. For thirty minutes we watched motorists speed past us. I cranked the starter a few more times, but with no results.

Just as Becky and Jo were ready to walk to the nearest house, a rusty Oldsmobile pulled in behind us. The man who emerged from the driver's seat had a light brown mustache and a goatee. He wore a greasy baseball cap, a well-worn leather jacket with the sleeves cut off at the shoulders, a red undershirt, and blue jeans. He looked like he should be riding a motorcycle with the Hell's Angels. When I glanced through the windshield of his car, I noticed a woman holding a little girl who couldn't have been much more than a year old.

"What seems to be the trouble?" the man asked.

I described our circumstances. He checked under the hood, then asked me to try cranking it over. More frustration. "I've got a buddy with a wrecker. I can call him on the CB if you want. His handle is Phantom. If he can't get your engine started, he can tow you into town for twenty-five dollars."

"That sounds great," I said, relieved that there was some hope in sight.

"Just one problem. There's only one gas station between here and Peru, and they're not open on Sundays. But the owner is a buddy of mine too. His CB handle is Pacemaker. Phantom and I both work for him. I'm sure he can get you back on the road tomorrow."

Suspicion slid into my consciousness. On the one hand, it sounded like a solid rescue plan. On the other hand, I had to wonder about this anonymous stranger who had such convenient connections. I decided to place my confidence in the Lord. After all, we couldn't stay on the road all night.

"I'd appreciate your help. My name is Bill Vamos."

He gave me a firm handshake. "I'm John Buchanan. My handle is Pinetree."

As we waited for Phantom, Pinetree and I became acquainted. He claimed that helping people was his favorite thing. "Folks think I'm crazy for doing stuff like this. And they're probably right." He laughed. "But I'm doing what I really want to do."

I had to admire this man.

While we chatted, Pinetree's wife stayed in the Oldsmobile, entertaining her little girl. My wife and children sat in our sedan, listening through the open windows. Finally, a tow truck pulled up and backed to within three inches of the front bumper. "Phantom" uncoiled his 230-pound frame from the truck, ambled to the open hood, and peeked inside. "You got an electronic ignition?"

My knowledge of cars would be appraised at about a preschool level. "No idea. It's a 1975 Chrysler. That's about all I know."

Phantom bent over the engine. "I can see the electronic ignition switch all right. That's probably where your trouble is. Those things are complicated."

I sighed. "Can you tow us into town?"

"Yeah. I can get you to Pacemaker's gas station."

"I'll follow you," Pinetree offered. "And then I'll take you to a motel for the night."

After the two men secured our car to the wrecker, my family got into the back seat of the Olds. I joined Phantom in the cab of the "green hook." The truck bounced and wove as it sped down the road. I held on tight.

Deciding this was a good time to make a new friend, I asked Phantom if he liked basketball. "My game's football," he said. "I used to be quick. At two hundred pounds, I ran the hundred-yard dash in 11.2 seconds. I was in track and shot put too. I came in second in the county."

Again, though for different reasons, I found myself impressed.

As the tow truck raced toward its destination, bucking my body so hard I half expected my spine to crack, we talked football and track, and he told me about his wife and three children.

When we reached the gas station, Pinetree pulled up behind us and jumped out of the car. "I just talked to Pacemaker. He says he thinks he knows what's wrong with your car. The electronic ignition switch is probably burned out. He says it happens all the time. There's an auto parts store open a few miles from here. If we can get the part, Phantom here could tow your car over to Pacemaker's house. He can work on it in his garage and maybe fix it tonight."

Seeds of doubt swept over me. Were all these coincidences too good to be true? I could see the headlines in my mind: *Pastor Duped by Con Men. Family Tortured and Killed in Back Alley.*

"I'll get on the CB and call the store," Pinetree offered. "Find out how much that part costs." He went to his car and came back a moment later. "The part is pretty expensive. Thirty-five bucks."

I had counted my money before leaving for the funeral. I had $72 in my wallet; $25 for the tow truck plus $35 for the part would leave me with $12. "What if it turns out I don't really need the part?"

Pinetree shrugged. "If you don't need it, you can return it to the store and ask for your money back."

It was no guarantee, but it was better than nothing. And at 7:15 p.m., we had already been delayed for nearly three hours.

Lord, if all this help is authentic, it's a miracle! If not, help us!

"Okay," I said. "Let's try it."

I endured a second ride in Phantom's overgrown steel-and-rubber bucking bronco, with our Chrysler still attached. After some slick maneuvering in the alley behind a garage that desperately needed a new coat of paint, Phantom unhooked the Chrysler from his tow truck, and I met a white-haired man in his fifties with a crew cut, who introduced himself as Pacemaker.

Phantom calculated his towing bill. Since he'd moved me twice, the total came to $27. I handed him the cash and thanked him several times. "Don't think anything about it. I do this day and night. It's my job."

He lingered a few minutes, then headed off as Pacemaker and Pinetree performed what looked like minor surgery on the Chrysler. Three more auto parts and an hour and a half later, I still wasn't sure whether anything productive was really happening.

At 9:05, Pacemaker asked me to crank the ignition . . . for what must have been the fortieth time. And when I turned the key, the engine roared into action. We all cheered and clapped. Then came the moment of truth. What would this stranger named Pacemaker charge me for four parts and hours of labor on a Sunday?

"How much do I owe you?" I asked, bracing myself.

"Nothing. I'm just sorry I took so long to fix your car."

Somehow, it made sense that a man who would allow his Sunday evening to be consumed by four marooned travelers would say that.

Jo and I protested. Finally, Pacemaker said with a grin, "If you two keep this up, you're going to make me mad."

"Yeah," Pinetree added. "Pacemaker is just that kind of guy."

The next Sunday I preached a sermon based on Luke 10:23–37.

"When Jesus was asked, 'Teacher, what shall I do to inherit eternal life?' he told the parable of the Good Samaritan. This story shows us the urgency of human need. But it also reveals that such need is the focus of eternal life.

"Jesus wasn't saying that if we do good deeds, we'll earn a berth in heaven. His point was that when you trouble yourself to meet the needs of another, you are participating in God's life on earth. And when heaven comes, you'll feel perfectly at home.

"Your encounters with life's weary travelers may come at the kitchen table, or during a coffee break in the office, from the people who cry out to you on the nightly news, or in the boardroom when you're helping to decide what your company will do about hiring minorities or how to make a profit and still serve people.

"Eternal life sometimes comes in unforgettable characters with names like Pinetree, Phantom, and Pacemaker. And in unforgettable people like you!"

2

A year after returning from sabbatical, I read an article in *Sojourners* magazine about the Church of the Savior in Washington, D.C. Its pastor, Gordon Cosby, believed that people desperately needed a deeper experience of faith than most churches were structured to offer.

Cosby saw the call to discipleship as an integration of two journeys: an inward journey of growth in love of God, self, and others, and an outward journey, helping to restore God's hurting people. He encouraged his congregation to consider how they might reach out to the world to help those who are broken. Small mission groups were formed, dedicated to various needs in the city of Washington and beyond. Since many of Cosby's beliefs reflected my own, I wanted to meet this man and visit his church.

Each year my congregation gave me a week off to upgrade my pastoral skills. When it was time for my study leave that year, I headed for Washington, D.C.

To my surprise, the Church of the Savior did not meet in a traditional church building. The members congregated in a small brownstone mansion for teaching and training. I attended a seminar at Dayspring, a lodge owned by the church at the periphery of two hundred acres of land dotted with lakes and trees. Pastor Cosby directed the seminar. In it, he integrated faith with caring for the world. He also urged taking time to play and making time for quiet. Play time and quiet time were definitely things I needed more of.

The next part of the seminar was a retreat from the busyness of the world, which we spent in silence, prayer, and Bible study. Later we all played croquet on the expansive lawn.

At the conclusion of the retreat I felt renewed.

Upon my return to Elkhart, I began to think about establishing a Renewal Center, patterned on the ideas I'd gleaned from the Church of the Savior. The teaching would revolve around helping people grow in Christ through prayer, Bible study, mutual support, physical refreshment, and caring for the world.

But soon after I resumed my duties at the Elkhart church, I realized that being a full-time pastor and establishing such a center would be too much for me. We had been in Elkhart almost ten years, and I felt it was time to evaluate where the next years would lead us. I wrestled with whether to stay in Elkhart, go to a larger church, or start the center.

I had become restless of late. And I'd heard that some people in the congregation wondered whether they should have a new pastor, since I wasn't working the long hours I had in the past. The timing for a change seemed right for me. Unfortunately, the timing was not right for my wife.

Chapter Twenty-Six

Jo

1

B ILL CAME HOME FROM THE RETREAT excited about what he had
experienced. When he expressed his desire to start a center
of his own, I thought it was a crazy idea. When he asked if I was
willing to leave Elkhart and the pastorate in order to start the
center, my first response was "No." Life was finally happy and
meaningful for me. And I didn't want to uproot our daughter Susan
and our son, Jeff, who was in his senior year of high school.

But as we were considering our options for the future, an
outspoken church member told me, "I believe it's time for a change.
We need a new pastor with lots of energy, someone who can stir
us up again."

I bit my tongue, not wanting her to see how hurt I was. *These
people will never find a pastor as capable and as gifted as Bill. And they
will certainly never find one who can preach as well as he does!* But having
dealt with this woman before on other issues, I knew there was no
way to change her mind.

Perhaps it was time to move after all.

I suggested to Bill that he consider getting a pastorate with a
larger congregation. After all, he was healthier than he'd ever been.
The lithium was doing its job. The doctor had assured us that Bill

was well. But my husband was lukewarm about the idea. And after careful consideration of the long hours involved in serving a larger congregation, I acknowledged that it was not a feasible alternative.

Bill had a strong passion for this new ministry. The retreats would provide a much-needed time of relaxation and rest for church officers, church staff members, married couples, singles groups, college students, and pastors. Knowing how little time these people had for solitude and prayer, I thought our retreats would give them an opportunity for meditation and reflection.

I could see why the idea of establishing a retreat center appealed to him. But I still had concerns. It would mean heading into unknown territory and starting a whole new life. I asked Bill if we could make it financially, and he said we would have funds from a grant for the first year and a half.

Torn between Bill's needs and mine, I asked, "Are you sure you want to do this?"

"Yes. I feel a strong calling to this ministry. It will be less taxing than a pastorate because I can set my own hours and work within my parameters, not the demands of the church."

I couldn't argue with that.

We started discussing where we wanted to live and where to locate the center. After long hours of research and consideration, we decided on Lafayette, Indiana. Bill wanted to remain in the state where he was known. He also liked the idea of staying near his presbytery.

Once we'd worked out the basic details, we approached our children with the idea. Becky was content at college at Hanover, Indiana, so our move wouldn't affect her. Jeff assured us he would be fine living at the Mennonite Biblical Seminary so he could stay behind to finish his senior year of high school. Susan said she was happy in Elkhart, but that she would enjoy a new adventure somewhere else. All the pieces seemed to be fitting together, so I finally told Bill, "Okay, let's give it a try."

When we told the church family about our decision to leave, there was a general feeling of sadness. Some expressed their thoughts in written notes and others in person, all conveying best wishes for the next phase of our lives.

Shortly after we announced to the presbytery that Bill was going to start a new ministry in Lafayette, we received a call from John Fall, a resident of West Lafayette who was on the board of directors of a retreat facility known as Leatherwood. He asked Bill if they could work together. A week later, Bill met John at Leatherwood, and after an intensive talk, they formed a partnership.

In his final sermon at Elkhart—most likely his final sermon anywhere—Bill said, "I really don't want to leave this dynamic, growing congregation. And no one wants to move from a place where life has been good and productive to a place where the future is uncertain. That's scary! But it is impossible for me not to follow my vision. For me, there is a much greater risk than embarking on a journey where no one else has blazed the trail. The greater risk would be not to begin the journey at all."

2

Lafayette, our new home, had much to offer. I liked the idea of being near Purdue University, with its many cultural advantages: concerts, lectures, and contact with people from all over the world. Chicago and Indianapolis were only a short drive away, allowing us more access to the cultural arts as well as great shopping.

Most of all, I loved the home we'd purchased—an 1860s Federal-style white-brick farmhouse that stood high on a hill overlooking the countryside, surrounded by walnut trees, on five and a half acres of land. We dubbed it "Singing Winds." About a mile to the west was a well-maintained cemetery, and to the east, about a half-acre down the hill, was a magnificent barn that was like a monument to the past. Susan was especially excited about the barn, which housed a horse that the previous owners allowed her to ride.

We moved in during early fall, when the trees were beginning to release their treasures of orange, gold, and brown. Walnuts dotted the land, and squirrels scampered everywhere. I felt a sense of peace and contentment as I walked the grounds. I had high hopes for a fresh, new, easier life in Lafayette.

Since I enjoyed people, making friends would be easy, I reasoned. But the first year after moving was excruciatingly difficult. Bill and I had left a city we loved, a lifestyle we'd known for twenty-two years, a position of high respect, and a congregation that valued our contributions and gifts. And I missed Jeff terribly. I felt adrift in uncharted waters.

I struggled to find a place in our new community, but a concatenation of disastrous events created tremendous obstacles. Our home in Elkhart didn't sell for a year. The previous owners of our new house refused to make any concessions to our needs. Becky had some health problems, with pain in her joints and accompanying fatigue, indicating that she might have lupus. Susan struggled to adjust to her new school.

To make matters worse, we couldn't find a church home. The gifts that had served me well in the past, like my singing voice, I perceived as not being needed or wanted where we now lived. Being so far out in the country, our social life was nonexistent.

The unrelenting stress took its toll on our marriage. I released my anger on Bill, blaming him for uprooting my life. I also turned my anger inward, resulting in many days of depression. In spite the pleasure of his work, Bill seemed lonely too, judging from the sadness I often saw in his eyes.

As our struggles threatened to tear us apart, an old demon surfaced: our disproportionate interest in sexual intimacy. Bill became more demanding, and I withdrew. We'd had some counseling over the years, and it had helped. So we visited Masters and Johnson, experts on sexual intimacy. They interviewed us, separately and together. They offered helpful suggestions to enhance romance. They gave us extensive counseling. Unfortunately, nothing worked.

Disappointed, puzzled, confused, and hurting, we allowed the topic of divorce to enter our conversations for the first time in our lives.

One day, as I was driving into town, late for an appointment, I was stopped by a slow train. "How can a city like Lafayette have tracks in the middle of town?" I wailed. I pounded the steering wheel, cursing the train as it rumbled its way across the intersection. Anger turned to tears, and then to a desperate prayer. "Why, God? Why are we here?"

I didn't get a response.

Even in the midst of my pain, I was relieved that Bill had found fulfillment in his new ministry. I wanted him to be happy.

Chapter Twenty-Seven

Bill

THE RETREAT CENTER BEGAN with a small core of people willing to work hard for what they believed. Eventually the word spread, and people began to show an interest in attending the retreats or becoming involved in the leadership.

As John Fall and I planned the first retreat, we learned that Leatherwood would not be available after all. So we held it at our farmhouse. Jo agreed to serve as hostess for the big event.

Nine men and women attended that first weekend retreat for a time of prayer, reflection, and relaxation. Jo enjoyed serving the meals because it provided an opportunity for her to meet new people. Most of the folks drove home on Saturday night, but a few spent the night at the farm house. At the end of the retreat I felt energized, believing this was what I had been called to do.

The retreats continued to meet at Singing Winds for another seven months, until we asked Sister Rita from upstate New York to direct an event as our first guest leader. After the retreat, she took me aside. "You can't keep doing this to your wife. Making meals, laundering sheets and towels, cleaning up after everyone leaves. Not to mention displacing the family from their rooms. You are going to have to find somewhere else to meet."

I had so much respect for Sister Rita and her expertise on spiritual retreats, I took her advice. After that, we met mostly in churches, in retreats around Lafayette and other parts of the country, and one year in a monastery.

As more people became involved in the work of the center, a board of directors was formed. The board discussed at length what to name the ministry, finally settling on the Center for Christian Growth. The board also developed guidelines for operations and articulated the main purpose for its existence: to help people develop communion with God and compassion for others.

We provided opportunities for mutual support by having individuals meet in small groups and relating their experiences, which helped build trust. We also had discussions about the importance of physical renewal, rest, nutrition, and exercise. And we encouraged the study of the Scriptures.

The retreat nurtured people, then sent them back into the world with greater compassion for their families, friends, and colleagues, and with the tools to enable them to express that love for others.

I'd never felt so satisfied.

Chapter Twenty-Eight

Jo

1

A S HE IMMERSED HIMSELF IN HIS WORK, Bill's frustration toward me dissipated. And as my husband's demeanor softened, so did mine. We ultimately abandoned the idea of divorce, realizing that we loved each other deeply and could never give up on our marriage. But I still felt lonely and isolated, living so far out in the country, with neighbors I hardly knew.

One warm summer morning, when Bill was in Florida leading a retreat, I folded clothes in the summer kitchen, enjoying the fragrance of freshly laundered clothes that had dried in the sunshine and lapsing into the memory of carefree days helping my mother when I was a child.

Suddenly Susan flew into the room, the screen door slamming behind her. "Mom," she yelled, "the bull has gotten out of the fence and is headed down the highway." Abandoning my laundry, I ran out the door, with Susan right behind. The bull we'd bought three months ago, in the hopes of it providing meat someday, had always been docile. *Maybe he's lonesome and needs some friends,* I thought with a wry chuckle as I ran around the side of the house.

Just past the garage, I saw a big, black four-legged blob ambling down the paved road in front of the house, cars honking and swerving to avoid hitting him. He seemed to be unaware of anything around him. How in the world was I going to get this one-and-a-half-ton animal back to the field? I couldn't push or pull the obstinate thing by myself.

When I passed our dog's food bowl, an idea came to me. *That's it!* I ran into the house and filled a huge pan with canned dog food. For extra incentive, I warmed it up. After throwing a few dog biscuits into the bowl, I hurried outside again. I told Susan to stay back, out of the way. Then I slowly approached the large animal, praying my idea would work.

I held the bowl close enough for the bull to smell, with honking cars swerving around us. When he started to nibble the warm dog food, I took a step backward. The bull followed, somehow avoiding the ongoing traffic. I could just imagine what people were thinking as they drove by. *What is that crazy lady doing?* But I didn't care. I had to concentrate on walking backward, holding a large bowl of dog food, with a bull trying to get to it, being careful not to stumble!

When we finally made it behind the fence, I scattered the dog food over the ground, ran for the gate, and quickly latched it behind me. Susan raced up to me. "Mom, are you all right?" After I assured her I was fine, we looked at the bull gobbling up dog food, and we burst into laughter.

2

Not long after moving into the farmhouse, I decided to do some remodeling. I hoped that would help me forget how lonely I was and how much I missed my friends in Elkhart.

I found some large pieces of stained glass in the barn that the previous owners had left behind and had them made into a window for the small downstairs bathroom. I learned how to wallpaper, and enjoyed giving the two small bathrooms and the upstairs bedroom a fresh, new look.

I also took voice lessons, and the farmhouse came alive with music. I joined the Bach Chorale Singers, a community musical group called Musicale, and Opera de Lafayette. During the summer, several churches asked me to sing for their worship services. I finally felt alive again, using a talent I had set aside while we moved and got settled in our new home.

As fall approached, I considered taking classes in sociology, counseling, and interior design at Purdue University. But when the time came to register, I was in North Carolina, visiting with my sister Ruth. When I told Bill, he signed me up for my classes. Since I didn't get back from my trip until after the first sociology lecture, Bill attended it for me. I loved this gift he gave me.

As soon as I returned from North Carolina, I began my studies. I was excited to be back in school and relished each course. My sociology class was huge, with more than two hundred young students. My interior design class wasn't nearly as easy as I'd expected. We had to learn how to design floor plans to scale, sketch in appropriate furnishings, and properly subdivide the available space. Then we had to defend our layouts in front of the class. My counseling class was delightfully easy. Having experienced much more of life than my fellow students gave me a distinct advantage. I entertained some thoughts of going for a degree in counseling. But whether that happened or not, my classes helped me find meaning for my life again.

3

I awoke one cold Saturday morning in January eager to climb out from under the warm blankets to share something with Bill. I was bursting with excitement as I bounded down the back stairs into the kitchen, where my husband was reading the newspaper. "I just had a very powerful dream!" I blurted out. Bill put down the paper. "We were all dressed up and going to a party. To get there, we had to climb some steep stairs. Others who were going to this event were in front of and behind us. But all of a sudden, the staircase just stopped." To give Bill a visual picture, I raised my arms, gesturing to the ceiling. "As we all stood there, wondering what to do, you disappeared. My mood changed from excited anticipation to panic, and I could sense the fear of other people around me. We were all questioning what to do. Some folks jumped into what looked like a lake. I considered doing the same, but something inside warned me to stay where I was. As terror and uncertainty threatened to envelop me, I felt a gentle hand on my shoulder, and I heard a voice say, 'I'm here, Jo. Everything will be all right.' I didn't know if it was the hand of God or your hand. But my fear fell away and I was at peace." I looked at Bill. "I know the dream means something important."

He got up from the kitchen table, walked over to where I stood, and smiled. "You look so happy, you're radiant." He kissed my forehead, then we embraced.

Life felt whole again.

4

Bill continued to find his work challenging and enjoyable. He carefully followed a healthy, balanced regimen of exercise, eating right, journaling, and spending time in prayer. He felt so physically and mentally healthy, the doctor decided to take him off his meds.

Bill did well . . . for a time. But two months after going off his meds, I noticed the warning signs that he was again slipping into a manic state. He insisted on having sex more frequently than I desired. He couldn't sleep, and, instead of becoming agitated, he ran up and down the stairs like a child, as if he were playing hide-and-seek. For the first time, Susan saw a manifestation of Bill's illness. With a maturity beyond her years, she accepted her father, even though she didn't recognize this strange person who'd taken over his body.

My heart sank with the realization that he needed to be hospitalized again. When I suggested this, he consented. He knew he needed help. Susan was trying to be brave as Bill and I headed for the hospital but soon little tears began to fall down her tiny cheeks.

His first week in the hospital, he paced endlessly in his room. Not wanting anyone to see him in this agitated state, for fear they would think less of him, I didn't tell anyone about his hospitalization. However, I visited him every day, hoping my presence would be helpful. His doctor put him back on his medication. Bill considered those meds a gift from God.

When he came home, after just a week and a half, Susan and I doted on him. I fixed his favorite meals, we played card and board games, I brought him coffee in bed. Bill loved all the attention, and soon he resumed his work at the center. He came home from each retreat full of excitement, sharing with me the satisfaction he experienced in his work.

Though our life had returned to a place of perceived normalcy, our issue with sexual intimacy still hung over us like an irritating odor. We had to deal with this once and for all. A friend of ours, Adreana, was getting her PhD in counseling and was skilled in understanding the complexities of sexuality in marriage. Bill and I were thrilled when she consented to take us on as clients, because we had great respect for her faith as well as her skills.

Our counseling sessions took place in Adreana's home. We met in what looked like a classroom, with a blackboard and charts. Bill and I sat in two chairs, nestled on comfortable pillows. Through the months that we worked with her, she helped us see that the culture and our families of origin had subtly preached the message that sex is wrong, something to be ashamed of. Our first experience with sex, on our wedding night, turned out to be painful and unfulfilled because we were both inexperienced. Whenever Bill went into a manic mode, his need for sex became more acute. And I became frightened.

As we delved deeper into the problem, I confessed to Adreana that Bill often told me, "I have a right to sex because you're my wife." I told her that made me feel like I had no rights.

Bill argued, "But I do have a right to—"

Adreana interrupted him with a soft retort. "No, Bill, you don't have a right to demand sex. Your demanding is actually a form of abuse."

He gasped as if she had punched him in the stomach. "I can't believe that. I would never abuse my wife." He gazed at me with agony in his eyes.

I had never thought of his demands for sex as abuse. But I said nothing. I felt a sense of relief, believing for the first time in this long journey that we were finally seeing the core of what needed to be healed.

When we returned home, the farmhouse was chilly. Bill started a fire in the wood-burning stove in the family room. While the flames crackled and blazed, he sat beside me on the sofa, looked at me, and then buried his head in my chest. "I am so sorry. I never intended to be abusive to you."

We talked well into the night. We'd had a similar talk in the past, but this time I felt like he was actually listening. I helped him realize that there were other ways to enjoy intimacy besides sex, little things that are meaningful to women. Like sitting by the fireplace, watching television together, or taking evening walks through the countryside.

His eyes sparkled with love for me. "I could learn how to cook and help you with the cleanup."

I smiled. "That would be great. But what I need most from you is patience in the bedroom."

He nodded. "I understand."

After that night, Bill never again made sexual demands on me. His transformation helped me relax, and I found myself wanting more sexual intimacy with this man I cared so deeply about.

5

Five and a half years after we moved into the farmhouse, Susan enrolled at Purdue University and began living in the dorm. With all three children out of the nest, the house that once felt like a refuge seemed deserted and empty. And I felt isolated. Even though Bill and I had come to enjoy our neighbors, most of our friends lived in West Lafayette.

I felt haunted by a sense that Bill and I needed to live closer to town, though I wasn't sure why. After considerable deliberation, we made the decision to move. We sold our house to a doctor and his family, knowing they would continue to take care of our beautiful home. We found a place in a friendly neighborhood of West Lafayette, with an unexpected bonus: an indoor swimming pool. Exercise was important to both of us, but especially to Bill, who found it a vital element in maintaining his mental balance and well-being.

The road we lived on was several miles long. Down the street from us were middle-class homes with children playing in the yards and basketball hoops hinged in front of garages. In the wooded area behind our home, the houses were larger and more ostentatious. Since we lived right in the middle of the neighborhood, I couldn't decide whether were we middle-class or among the upper crust.

6

A year after our move to West Lafayette, I discovered a nodule on my breast while taking a shower. I wondered if I should make an appointment with the doctor. But before I had a chance to decide, my brother-in-law Norm called and told me that my sister Lois, who had been battling breast cancer for eight months, didn't have long to live. I knew I needed to go to California to say good-bye.

Bill made plane reservations for me while I packed, and we drove to the airport early the next morning. Before I left, he said he would pray for us.

During the plane ride to California I recalled moments when my life intersected with Lois's. She was eleven years older than I was, and while I was still in high school she was the mother of two daughters. With her dimpled cheeks, pug nose, and pixie-like personality, Lois endeared herself to everyone who knew her. Her heart was soft and welcoming. I remembered one Christmas, when Ruth and I were students at Berea and Lois invited us to spend the holidays with her family. She didn't complain when Ruth and I slept until noon while she worked hard cooking and cleaning.

Norm picked me up at the airport. As he drove to the house, we talked about our grown children and about Lois. When Norm pulled into the driveway, Lois opened the front door. My heart sank as I gazed at her once-beautiful body, now shriveled away. I hugged her gently, afraid she might break. She put on a brave face, trying to hide her pain. I followed her as she walked slowly down the hall to her room. As she slipped into bed, I asked what I could do to help.

"I'm hoping you can give me a bath after I get some rest. That would give Norm a break."

Though this seemed an odd request, I replied, "Of course."

While she napped, I cleaned up the kitchen and Norm caught up on paperwork for his jewelry business. When Lois called out that she was awake and in the bathroom, I responded immediately and joined her there. Her frail body writhed in pain as I helped lower her into the warm soothing water in the tub. But Lois didn't complain. That wasn't her way. She put a bright face on everything. We even laughed at the little sprouts of hair that were beginning to spike upward on her bald head, a result of months of chemotherapy.

Since it took a lot of energy for her to talk, there was little verbal interaction between us. While I washed her back, I thought about the nodule I had discovered in my breast. Did I also have cancer? Strangely, I felt no fear of the possibility. Though I couldn't explain why, I had the feeling that I would be all right no matter what. I put thoughts of myself aside as I helped Norm with his chores around the house. I made meals, changed bedding, and vacuumed the floors.

At Norm's request, I painted the peeling baseboards in the small guest bathroom. As I sat on the floor, painting behind the toilet, my arm brushed against my breast, which felt tender. I felt again for the lump. *Dear God, please don't let it be breast cancer!*

At the end of the week, I flew home and immediately made an appointment with my ob-gyn. The mammogram confirmed what I had feared. I had every right to be terrified. But I was not going to let this news defeat me. I had been through a lot in my life already. What was a little cancer?

At my next visit with the ob-gyn, I received news that stunned me. Three nodes were affected, requiring a mastectomy and eight months of chemotherapy, which would result in nausea, loss of hair, and severe fatigue.

In spite of this devastating diagnosis, the possibility of death never entered my mind. I still had a lot to live for. As a matter of fact, I believed that a new and better chapter in my life lay ahead. But Bill was gripped with guilt, believing the stress caused by our fights over our sexual differences had caused the cancer. I tried to reassure him that it wasn't his fault, but my words fell on deaf ears.

He called Adreana, our counselor, and told her how he felt. "Guilt doesn't achieve anything," she reminded him. Bill internalized those words and eventually let go of the guilt.

7

As I underwent the mastectomy and eight months of chemotherapy, food became my enemy. I felt nauseated almost all of the time. Prayer was a constant balm that helped heal our physical and emotional beings. Bill and I grew closer, promising each other new commitments of love.

When I finally finished my treatments and regained my strength, Bill took me on a cruise to the Caribbean to celebrate. With chemotherapy behind me, I was free to eat whatever I wished—and I did! At one meal, the waiter laughed as he placed a seventh dessert in front of me and I downed every bite.

On most days, we sat on the deck, reading, praying, and sunning ourselves. All around us, the sea rocked us gently with sun-tipped waves. Much of that time I questioned where life was going to take me next. Surely cancer had lessons to teach me, which I hoped to be able to pass on to others.

Soon after we returned home from the cruise, a woman named Shirley called. She told me she was in remission from breast cancer and was the director of a program started by the American Cancer Society called Reach to Recovery, where women in remission visited with other women right after their surgeries. She asked if I might be interested in working with them. I wanted to know more, so Shirley and I met for lunch. As she talked, I knew this was what I wanted to do.

After six months of training at the headquarters of the American Cancer Society—and waiting for my hair to grow back—I began visiting women in hospitals and in their homes, giving them literature from the cancer society with suggestions about exercises, how to care for their incisions, and more. I also listened to their concerns and responded based on my personal experiences and what I'd learned from the ACS.

Many women told me that their biggest encouragement was seeing someone who had been through cancer doing so well. These visits also enriched me, because I believed I had played a part in their healing. On one of those occasions, I met Eleanor, who had recently been divorced and was working on her graduate degree in social work. As soon as she was well enough, she planned to continue her studies. We had a cordial visit, and when it was time to leave, I wondered if I would ever see her again.

A month later Eleanor called, very excited. "My dissertation is going to be about support groups. Would you help me start one for women with breast cancer?"

My heart raced with excitement. "When do we start?"

Eleanor and I found a church downtown that agreed to let us meet there. Then we worked hard to get the word out that there was a support group for women affected by breast cancer, a place where they could get together with others, share their fears, receive encouragement, and provide and share advice.

At our first meeting, five vulnerable but determined women sat around an old wooden table in that church, talking about their lives and their fears about their breast cancer. In the ensuing months, more women joined our group. Soon the old wooden table wasn't big enough, so we started meeting at the YWCA.

The support group taught me not to be afraid to ask for help when I needed it. I knew that maintaining a positive attitude was important, but I learned that it was OK to be angry, even with God, about having cancer.

In the support group we found interesting ways to survive our chemo treatments, like visualizing the white cells in our bodies killing the cancer cells. This proved to be an effective relaxation technique. The support group also encouraged us to heal from the emotional wounds of our past, to deal with those things that we needed to forgive, and to close the book on any unfinished business in our lives.

One woman who visited the group for the first time said, "I was diagnosed with advanced breast cancer, and the doctor gave me six months to live. That was nine years ago!"

After we all rejoiced together, I asked, "Why do you think you're still living after such a bleak diagnosis?"

She told us about her daughter, who had some serious health concerns. "I'm convinced I'm still here because my daughter needs me."

People started calling to ask if I would speak at churches and women's organizations about our support group and how cancer had impacted my life. I shared with them the life changes I'd had to make, and the importance of loving and nurturing ourselves by keeping our immune system healthy by getting enough exercise, eating healthy foods, and giving ourselves permission to retreat regularly for rest and prayer. I also told them how I'd dealt with stress by not letting small annoyances upset me. The trials of cancer gave me the empathy to understand other people's pain. I joined a Christian lay counseling ministry in my church. Women of all ages shared their struggles with me. I was careful not to preach or tell them what to do. I just listened.

These ministries made me feel like my life had meaning again. And Bill was thankful that I'd found fulfillment.

8

In October 1993, the tree-lined streets of West Lafayette were awash with yellow, red, and orange leaves. When winter snow blanketed the world around us, the smell of wood burning in fireplaces reminded me that change is always just around the corner—whether we're prepared for it or not.

On Saturday, October 4, Bill and I were getting ready to attend a cocktail party at the home of a couple who lived a quarter of a mile down the hill from us. Knowing that many interesting and important people would be there, I wore a simple aqua dress and jacket, with matching heels. Bill put on a light brown suit and a yellow tie, accentuating his neatly trimmed beard and tanned face. As we walked out the door, I thought I had never seen my husband look so handsome and well. He had been complaining of pain in his upper right femur for the past several weeks, presumably from a pulled muscle. Did he have pain that night, I wondered.

For me, parties were like treasure hunts. I enjoyed searching for hidden jewels that reflected a person's life and history. Everyone has a story to tell, and I wanted to know at least a part of it. The more people I conversed with, the happier I felt.

Bill never enjoyed cocktail-party chatter. He was content to find one or possibly two people with whom to hold an in-depth conversation.

At the party that night, Bill carried on a lengthy discussion about theology with Mary Jo, one of our neighbors. He was animated and clearly happy, and I was relieved that he had found someone to talk with. But I noticed he was sitting when almost everyone else was standing. I knew then he must be hurting.

The pain in Bill's leg forced him to see his doctor for a physical exam and a blood workup. To our surprise, the nurse called that afternoon, saying the doctor wanted to see him the next day. That concerned me, so I went to the appointment with him.

The waiting room was full of patients, but eerily silent. Some folks read while others dozed. Most people stared into space, lost in their thoughts. Bill and I found a place to sit and chatted quietly with each other about the cocktail party and our plans for the rest of the day. Before long the nurse called Bill's name and led us into the doctor's office. She told us to be seated, then asked Bill the usual questions.

The office, which was five degrees colder than most rooms, and smelled of disinfectant, reminded me of the day eight years earlier when I was told that I had breast cancer. I prayed we wouldn't hear similarly devastating news about Bill.

After filling out the paperwork, the nurse informed us that our regular doctor was out of town but his partner would be with us shortly. Fifteen minutes later, a tall man with graying hair walked in. He introduced himself as Dr. Kerry, shook hands with both of us, and sat behind his desk. After briefly studying a file, he turned to Bill. "Your PSA number is 6.5. A normal reading is anywhere between zero and two."

Bill blinked. "What does that mean? What's a PSA?"

"It's a test that determines whether or not a person has prostate cancer. Your number is extremely high, which means you have stage-four cancer." There was no empathy in his voice, nothing resembling compassion after having just handed my husband a death sentence.

Bill and I gasped. How could this be? He had taken such good care of himself. Running almost every day, eating well . . .

"I'm sending you to the hospital for further tests. The lab technicians will be waiting for you." He shook our hands and walked out the door.

Bill and I sat in stunned silence. His mouth opened, but no sound came out. My hand covered my chest as if trying to help my heart start beating again.

Finally, Bill stood and reached for my hand. "Let's head for the hospital." As we drove there, a feeling of numbness set in. I had read about the stages of grief. Denial was the first. I needed to concentrate on the task at hand.

As we walked into St. Elizabeth Hospital, I wondered if Dr. Pennington might be there. He'd been my oncologist eight years ago, and I highly respected him for his professionalism and for his faith.

As a nurse escorted us to the lab, I saw Dr. P. I dropped Bill's hand, ran down the corridor, and threw my arms around my old friend. "What are you folks doing here?" he asked.

I told him about Bill's PSA number, and the doctor who didn't seem to care, and asked if he could help us.

"You know, I'm not ordinarily at the hospital at this time. My normal hours are later in the day. I believe it was in God's plan that I'd be here just when you need me."

I couldn't have agreed more!

He made arrangements for Bill to be admitted to the hospital to begin treatments that very day.

After he was comfortably situated in his hospital bed, I followed the nurse out of the room. Hoping for a word of encouragement, I asked her how long she thought Bill had to live. She seemed reluctant to give me a definitive answer, but I begged her, assuring her that I could handle the news, whatever it was. "Around three months," she finally replied.

That's not long enough!

When the nurse headed for her station, I found a quiet corner in the hall and sank into one of the chairs. I didn't want to lose my husband now that we had discovered such a sweet and deep love for each other. The albatross around our necks had been released and we'd been flying free. Our best years together were still ahead of us.

I thought of ways to fight for my husband's life. The best things I could think of were to cook nutritious foods that would nourish his body and to help him revisit people and places that he loved. I'd also have to put on a brave face and concentrate on the tasks at hand. Bill needed my strength.

When I visited him, he expressed concern that he might slip into another episode. I called for Dr. Ram, his psychiatrist, and asked if he could visit Bill in the hospital. Though he seemed reluctant at first, he finally agreed to come the next morning. He arrived while Dr. Pennington was in the room, talking with us about Bill's treatments. The minute he walked in the room. I saw relief on Bill's face. Dr. Ram nodded to me and shook hands with Dr. Pennington.

My brain went into mental overload while the two doctors talked with my husband and me. But in the midst of the blur of conversation, Dr. Ram's voice cut through the haze. "If you had performed your wifely duty, this might not have happened."

I stood there in shocked silence. Dr. Ram had no idea about the long journey we had traveled. As if I hadn't piled enough guilt on myself through the years . . . before Bill and I learned those important insights that finally conquered the savage beast.

A long moment of icy silence followed. Then the conversation continued. But I didn't hear a word of it.

In the days that followed, doctors, nurses, lab technicians, and chaplains paraded in and out of the hospital room. Visitors also came, most unable to express their feelings or afraid they might say the wrong thing. I empathized with their struggle and found myself comforting them with hugs and words of reassurance.

After a few days of lab tests and medications, Bill was released. We knew his time was limited, so we were determined to live our lives to the fullest. The first thing we did to celebrate was head to Arnie's for Bill's favorite pizza.

Days melted into weeks, and winter winds played upon window panes, soon replaced by warm summer breezes. Bill continued to improve. His PSA numbers receded and the pain he'd been experiencing since October abated. Life became a precious gift. Cancer was still attacking his body, but Bill felt reasonably healthy.

Nothing was more important to my husband than touching the lives of those closest to him. Becky had married and became the mother of two little girls. Jeff was also married and had a baby boy. We'd been wanting for a long time to visit Jeff and his family in California. Because of the distance, we had put it off. Now there were no more excuses.

Their modest ranch home was located in a busy neighborhood, and in the backyard they had a garden with flowers growing among tomato plants. Inside the house were beautiful pieces of furniture that Jeff had made: a roll-top desk, a dining-room set, and a coffee table. I was delighted that Jeff had continued the hobby he began in high school.

I was especially thankful that Bill was able to spend time with his son and daughter-in-law. We had a cookout in the backyard and visited the church where Jeff was associate pastor. We didn't talk about anything deep or serious, just enjoyed our time together. Bill was feeling so well, it was easy to forget the battle that lay ahead.

When we returned home, his strength and energy began to diminish. The doctor encouraged him to relinquish his duties with the Center for Christian Growth. Bill continued leading retreats, but made preparations to turn over his work to one of his colleagues.

The whole family came to our home for Christmas. Tears abounded. There were no purchased gifts, only homemade ones from the heart. We each gave Bill presents that we hoped would have special meaning for him: poems, letters of love, goodies from the kitchen, hand-knitted socks.

Bill's gifts to the family were written declarations of love. Few things in my life carry the emotional impact as the piece he wrote for me, which he titled "My Rainbow Person."

How do I write about a rainbow person in my life? Words can't come close to describing a rainbow that must be seen by the heart as well as the eyes, and touched by the spirit, and smelled like the aroma of fresh rainfall on thirsty grass. Yes, my rainbow person moves from thunderstorm to calm, because her life has been full of turbulence. She takes darkness and heavy clouds and transforms them with her tears, her determination, and her creativity. Her devotion and prayers have saved my life, and her tears keep reminding my heart of how precious love can be.

Tears spilled down my cheeks as I read those words. I reached for his hand and gently kissed it.

The pieces he wrote for every member of the family painted a picture of love and caring. We all wept, knowing we would never celebrate another Christmas with this special man.

As Bill's health declined, the entire family returned to the Upper Peninsula of Michigan, where we'd spent our happiest days. We rented the cabin closest to the lake, the one Bill's parents had always rented when he was growing up. Happy memories flooded in when we walked inside—days of fishing, meals of northern pike, card games after dinner, and lots of time for ourselves and each other. Bill spent much of his time sitting on the beach overlooking the waters of Lake Huron. There the sunshine warmed his frail body while the grandchildren played around him in the sand.

He wanted to make one more trip, to attend our family reunion. Every two years, our extended family of around seventy people met for an entire week. We always participated in various fun activities: sports, picnics, a talent show, a women's book group, art lessons, sign-language instructions. Bill and I enjoyed as many of the activities as we could. But the most important part of the week was getting reacquainted with members of our family.

When we returned from the reunion, Bill was anxious to see his close friends and say good-bye to them. I called each one and scheduled a time for them to visit. Some of Bill's clergy colleagues were reluctant to talk about anything that would remind him of his death. They joked and made small talk. But Bill was eager to share with them what he was experiencing, so he managed to direct the conversations to what he considered important: his death and his faith. He told me he found it helpful to talk openly with his friends and colleagues, and he believed it was healing for them as well.

The children took turns talking with their father. In a slow, deliberate voice, he spoke to them about the standout moments in their lives that he remembered. Sitting next to him on the bed, they recounted happy memories of times they'd spent with him. As I listened nearby, tears clouding my swollen eyes, I took notes, not wanting to forget those precious moments.

Bill's pain became so great, he found walking difficult. Even going to the bathroom was an ordeal. So I ordered a hospital bed, which I placed next to mine. The doctor prescribed heavy doses of pain medication.

I needed support as well, so I called hospice. It was a relief to have a nurse, a social worker, and volunteers come to the house. Dr. Pennington visited several times and seemed pleased that Bill was resting in a bright and cheerful room full of sunlight.

As Bill's primary caregiver, I was pretty much homebound, except when a hospice volunteer stayed with him so I could run errands. Friends often dropped by to visit with me. I always asked them to pray that Bill would not suffer.

One morning in October, Bill told me, "You know, Jo, I have very little pain." I knew God was answering those prayers.

In early November, our daughter Becky dropped by with my longtime friend Lynn, who lived in Indianapolis. We talked and played games next to Bill's bed so he would know we were near.

About a week into their visit, we ordered pizza for dinner. When the doorbell rang, Becky and Lynn ran downstairs to answer. I kissed Bill's cheek and said we would be back as soon as we'd finished our meal.

While we were eating, we heard a crashing noise upstairs, as though something had fallen over. We ran back to Bill's room. He had slipped into a peaceful, eternal sleep. There were no more tears, only relief that he was no longer suffering. In my heart I wondered what had caused the crashing noise that had brought us running.

Guilt haunted me for not having been present when my husband died. This continued until the hospice social worker told me that people often choose to die when their loved ones are out of the room.

Years later a well-known authority on grief spoke to our women's group at church. She talked about people reaching out for a loved one when they're dying, and I wondered if the noise I'd heard when Bill died might have been caused by his reaching for me. I found comfort in the belief that the hand of God had reached down for his servant Bill.

9

The day before the funeral, the Hippensteel Funeral Home in downtown Lafayette held a visitation. Hundreds of people stood in a line that snaked around the large reception room, waiting to extend their love and condolences to our family. My children stood at my side, while my two young granddaughters scampered about, enjoying the attention. I repeatedly assured folks that Bill had experienced very little pain during his illness, and that I would make it.

After two hours, I encouraged my family to take a break. They scattered to get something to eat. I slipped off my shoes and dug my toes into the soft nylon carpeting. As I was enjoying a moment of quiet introspection, Jurgen Honig came into the reception room.

George, as I called him, had attended several seminars that Bill had led at his church. But I had only met him twice.

The first time was at a Christmas party at our home in West Lafayette, when Bill and I hosted my Purdue Women's Short Story Book Club in 1987. George's wife, Trudy, was its organizer and facilitator. I was surprised when she asked me to join, because neither Bill nor I were on the faculty at Purdue University. "You'll just have to be an illegitimate member," Trudy joked.

Members and their spouses had gathered in our family room later that year, and the following Christmas as well, to exchange books and enjoy each other's company. On both occasions I spoke only briefly with George. Two years slipped away before I saw him again. His wife, Trudy, had passed away six months before, after a long illness.

George expressed his deep sadness for my loss, and I knew he understood. I asked him how he found out about the visitation. He said, "Every Wednesday morning, Faith Presbyterian Church has a prayer service. I play a brief organ prelude at the beginning. After the meeting yesterday, I overheard some women talking about Bill. When I heard the visitation was taking place this afternoon, I decided to come and pay my respects."

He touched my arm and looked me in the eye. "Jo, after enough time has gone by, would you mind if I called and invited you to have dinner with me?"

Without hesitation, I said yes. I could make a new friend and get a free dinner at the same time. What did I have to lose?

10

Solemn organ music played softly in the background as the children and I entered the church for Bill's funeral. While people gathered in the sanctuary, we sat silently in the parlor, waiting for the service to begin.

After everyone else had been seated, the ushers led us to the front pew. I prayed for Becky, who had decided only two hours before the service to say something about her father. She adored her father and was easily brought to tears. I wondered if she would break down in the middle of her talk and not be able to recover.

Three pastors conducted the service, each one painting a picture of a life lived with integrity and bravery. When it was Becky's turn to speak, she stood at the front of the sanctuary, her dark brown hair softly framing her radiant face. "I remember my father's embracing arms and his gentle, caring heart," she said. Her voice was strong, without even a tiny waver in it. "Dad was a joyful spirit who freely gave his love and who graciously accepted love from others. Even when he was dying and it was difficult for him to communicate, some of his last words to me were 'Are you all right?'"

As she continued speaking, I saw a translucent figure in white standing in front of Becky. Was it Bill's spirit there to uphold her, to give her strength? As soon as she finished her speech, the figure vanished. Becky rejoined the family, sitting next to me. I put my arm around her and pulled her close. How proud I was of my firstborn!

My husband's longtime friend Ron Elly took the platform next. "Bill knew no enemies," he said. "He saw the good in everyone and in every situation. His life was lived with meaning and purpose. He looked for the positives while acknowledging the shadows. Even his struggles with bipolar limitations served as grist for his preaching, teaching, and healing of others."

I gulped. Now everyone knew about Bill's disorder! I wondered what people in the congregation thought. Then I heard a voice in my spirit saying, *It's time, Jo. Time to let the truth be known.* The divine assurance instantly calmed my soul.

"Bill served three parishes," Ron continued. "A country church and two city churches. Everywhere he went, he used his gifts of preaching, counseling, and administration. But he didn't neglect his ministry to the community and the world. He served on the school board, worked for decent housing for disadvantaged people, and strove for justice and racial reconciliation."

I had always been proud of how my husband had cared about the world with such deep compassion.

"I remember well Bill's spirituality," Ron continued. "His prayer, silence, and solitude. His creative thinking and reading. His physical exercise and his mutual support. He empowered others to lead in the ministry of the Center for Christian Growth. During the last days of his illness, a friend wrote a letter to Bill which he showed to me. I kept it so I could share it with you today." He pulled a piece of paper from his pocket and read: 'All the wonder, wisdom, and compassion you poured on me! You were an anchor and a port when I needed it the most. I wondered why you had to suffer so much. I guess God saw that you were strong and a saint and could handle it, especially with your heart for prayer.'"

Tears trickled down my face. It seemed so unfair that Bill had suffered so much in this life. But the Lord had used even his suffering to bless others. Ron's eyes misted as he put the paper back in his pocket. "Bill had a wonderful sense of humor. He loved to laugh. With twinkling eyes and a knowing smile, he lived life with *oomph!* But he was never afraid to show tears, especially when his children sang or ran cross-country." I chuckled, remembering those happy times of musicals and running all over the state to attend Jeff's meets. "Bill chose joy even in his suffering," Ron said. "His life and ministry impacted many lives. But I imagine his children would say that his greatest accomplishment was being a dad, sharing with them his humor, his time, and his love."

Yes, despite being born bipolar, my husband had lived a full, productive, influential life. He loved and was loved. And though at times our struggles seemed insurmountable and life was excruciatingly painful, through faith, perseverance, and love, we made it!

Ron opened the Bible on the podium and read one of Bill's favorite Scripture passages, 1 Corinthians 13:8. "Love knows no limit to its endurance, no end to its trust. It is, in fact, the one thing that still stands when all else has fallen" (Phillips).

It was true. With everything that our family had been through, love stood strong: my love for Bill and his love for me and his family.

After the service, friends, family, and other loved ones gathered in the fellowship hall for a reception. As they shared memories of Bill and surrounded me and my children with words of encouragement and love, I felt oddly at peace. Every morning for the past thirteen months, ever since Bill received his diagnosis, I had sat in our family room, in front of the picture window overlooking the ravine, and prayed, "I'm trusting You, God." I cooked healthy meals, hoping to prolong Bill's life. We spent time talking, so that nothing would be left unsaid when the time came. I had said and done everything I needed to say and do. I had no guilt or regrets. I was just grateful for the time I had with him.

Now I was ready to let go and move on with my life.

11

A few weeks after Bill's funeral, one of our pastors asked if I would be willing to help her coordinate a counseling outreach program for members of the church, called Stephen Ministry. I wanted to stay busy, so I eagerly said yes. Buried in the preparations, I had little time to think of anything else.

Two months after Bill's funeral, George Honig called and invited me to dinner. On our first date, he did all the right things. He brought flowers, took me to one of the premier restaurants in the community, and ordered fine wine. He charmed me with his German accent and his sophistication.

I knew very little about George, except that he was a member of the faculty in the Department of Chemistry at Purdue, so I spent most of our evening asking questions. To my surprise we had a lot of things in common. He had been to India numerous times, speaking at the Institute of Science in Bangalore as well as other locations. He played the organ, so music was another common denominator. We had both grown up in multiple countries— George in Germany, Turkey, and the United States, and I in Africa, India, and the United States. During our grade school and high school years, we had both attended boarding school. Of course, we also had our differences. George was an introvert who loved math and science. I enjoyed the arts and being around people.

As the evening progressed, I felt more and more at ease with George. Being with him felt natural. His jokes suggested that he was comfortable with me too. By the end of our date, I no longer thought of him as a new friend but as someone I could seriously care about.

Over the next several months, in spite of our busy schedules, we spent many evenings together, getting better acquainted. During those days, I remembered the dream I'd had several years before, the one where Bill disappeared and then a gentle hand rested on my shoulder, reassuring me that I would be safe. When I had shared my dream with Bill, we saw it as a promise of hope, that even in the midst of all the hardships in life we had the assurance that God still walked with us. I now wondered if that dream had been a foreshadowing of Bill's death, with the promise from God that I would ultimately be all right. I believed Bill would have wanted me to move on, to begin the next chapter of my life.

In early April, as I worked on my presentation for Stephen Ministry in my living room, the doorbell rang. I wondered who was stopping by for a visit. When I opened the door, I saw a delivery man holding a vase filled with a dozen red roses. I thanked him, then hurried inside to read the card. My hands shook as I tore open the envelope and read, "Jo, I love you. George."

I gasped. I knew I loved him, but he had given no indication of deep feelings toward me, and I'd wondered if he felt the same about me. Now I had the answer!

I immediately called him, but no one answered. I left a message, thanking him enthusiastically for the flowers. As I waited for him to phone me back, I wondered what had brought about this sudden and unexpected display of emotion and romance. Could this be his way of asking me to marry him? If it was, I knew my answer would be yes.

When he returned my call, he told me, "Ever since I laid eyes on you at the first Christmas party at your home, I was smitten by you. I told no one. But the other day, it hit me. We've only been dating for a few months, but I don't have time to waste wondering if you love me or whether I should look elsewhere. I took a chance and sent you the roses and the note declaring my love. I was enormously relieved when you left a message thanking me. It gave me hope that you would accept what I intended as a proposal."

Like George, I had no interest in wasting time. Setting everything else aside, including my work with the Stephen Ministry, we went about buying rings, making wedding preparations and honeymoon plans, selling our homes and buying a new one, and planning a trip to India, where he would be lecturing at the Institute of Science.

George and I married on August 12, 1995, surrounded by close friends and family, in a little white church in the countryside. Halfway through the service, when Pastor Stuart was praying for us, I thought, *Bill would approve of this kind and gentle man of principle. George will be my safe harbor, a buffer against the unpredictability of life.*

When we recited our vows, "to have and to hold from this day forward," everyone present shed tears of joy.

Epilogue

My life was enriched by marrying Bill Vamos. I had no doubt that God had chosen Bill for me. There was a love and trust between us so deep that even his bipolar disorder could not tear us apart.

Bill taught me how to live even in the midst of suffering, and how to persist in attaining a life of meaningful fulfillment: trusting God, loving our family, and having compassion for the suffering of our world. He had lived his life in undeniable proof that, even in the face of great suffering, each individual life has value, purpose, and beauty.

Acknowlegements

As I reflect upon my journey in writing this book, I begin by remembering those who profoundly touched and influenced Bill's life and mine:

Our parents, who loved us unconditionally.

Our three churches, that nurtured, loved, and respected Bill.

Our children, who adored their father.

I am indebted to the many people who offered help and guidance after Bill died and the time came to finish writing his manuscript. The support, patience, and careful editing of my friends Kathy Ide and Roben Smith gave life to the manuscript and motivated me to keep writing.

Even before I had finished the manuscript, my life-long friends Lynn Roberts and Eleanor Pershing asked to read the draft. I am enormously grateful for their supportive and encouraging responses, which inspired me to continue.

I owe a huge debt of gratitude to the friends who graciously consented to read the finished manuscript and provided helpful input. Many thanks to Professor of Psychological Sciences Jerry Gruen, Professor of Communications Glenn Sparks, Cheri Sparks, Pastor Stuart Robertson, Ingrid Cleaver, Carol Fillmore, Jean Peterson, Sherry McCutcheon, Anne Hunt, and Paula Leirpertz.

I would be remiss if I did not thank the staff of White River Press—Linda Roghaar, Kitty Florey, and Margaret Gyorgy—who graciously guided me through the publication process.

But I owe my greatest thanks and gratitude to my husband Jurgen (George) Honig, who has walked hand in hand with me through this process. George's helpful criticism has been the spark that kept me going to the finish line.

CPSIA information can be obtained
at www.ICGtesting.com
Printed in the USA
LVHW090922310721
694223LV00004B/398

9 781887 043656